AFTER

BLACK

COFFEE

━━━◆━━━

BY

ROBERT I. GANNON, S.J.

PRESIDENT OF FORDHAM UNIVERSITY

THE DECLAN X. McMULLEN COMPANY

NEW YORK

CONTENTS

TO NON-IRISHMEN

TO FELLOWMEN

TO HIS EMINENCE

FRANCIS CARDINAL SPELLMAN

PREFACE

"After Black Coffee" this evening in thousands of hotels
and clubs all over the country, a toastmaster will rap for
order, and the diners, who up to that moment have been
enjoying themselves, will turn toward the dais with a
gentle, beaten look. Nobody will want to hear a speech,
nobody will know why every dinner has to be ruined by
having them, but it is part of the great American ritual and
has to go on—and on.

The ancestry of the after-dinner speech is supposed to
derive from the minstrelsy of the earliest times, which was
also interminable. It seems more likely, however, that it is
a degenerate form of good after-dinner conversation, which
is, of all earthly things, the most rare and the most delight-
ful. Even in the golden age of Chauncey M. Depew, when
the rules were already hardening and men arose to speak
lined with oysters, terrapin, pheasant and beef washed
down with five or six wines, they were still expected to be
light, informal, as casual as a boy in the Cambridge Union.
Important things were to be said, of course, but almost as
obiter dicta. The secret was to get the audience laughing
and, when their mouths were open, to throw them a thought
to chew on. All the average diner was expected to take
away besides a general sense of well-being was one definite
impression and a few good phrases. So that the speaker
worked almost as hard on the impression and the phrases
as he did on the essential spontaneity. He had to say in
minutes what a lecturer in the university would fondle for
an hour, and say it with such effect that his hearers would
go away convinced that the message was not only concise,
positive and colorful but, in spite of rhetorical exaggeration, true. Of course, not everyone in the nineties was a

Chauncey M. Depew, but the fact that a speaker had to stand in his own place without a reading desk or an amplifier did tend to limit the field and discourage many men of action from attempting the impossible.

Today, however, a big formal dinner is a dreadful experience. The toastmaster, whose only legitimate function is to break down the natural prejudice which an audience feels toward the next speaker, frequently makes the principal speech before introducing him. Then the speaker, who has been chosen because of his success in some other field, retires behind a stockade of microphones, whips out a manuscript—and as very few people read well, the rest can be imagined.

Here, then, are a few such manuscripts, offered as a study in American social customs. They are of two kinds. Some, like those for the Pan American Society and the Friendly Sons, were written out beforehand for the radio. Some, like those before the Chamber of Commerce and the Bar Association, were taken down by stenographers and afterwards translated into English. That was hard enough on the desired spontaneity, but when the publisher gathered them together from various sources it was discovered that, like some wines, humor and local color do not always "travel." The sallies that are a huge success in the heat of the moment and are followed in the record by "(laughter and prolonged applause)" are frequently flat, when they are not objectionable, in cold print. Unfortunately, in the process of removing the stale asides, some speeches were washed out altogether and their places had to be taken by two that were actually given before dinner.

The most persistent themes presented here in various guises are those that seem most appropriate in the present crisis: the dignity of man as a spiritual being and the importance of tradition in maintaining, or better, in regaining, our way of life. While these themes can hardly be overemphasized, presented in one book for one reader they can be tiresome. It might be well if they were read one or two at a time after black coffee.

TO BUSINESS MEN

PLATO'S GARDEN AND THE REDS
Address at the Dinner of the Real Estate Board of the State of New York, February 1, 1941

AN EDUCATIONAL PROGRAM FOR THE UNITED STATES
Address at the 172nd Annual Banquet of the Chamber of Commerce of the State of New York, November 14, 1940

PEACE THROUGH BUSINESS
Address at the Farewell Luncheon to the Members of the International Business Conference, November 20, 1944

PLATO'S GARDEN

AND THE REDS

———◆———

I CAME HERE TONIGHT
PARTLY BECAUSE I AM
IN NEED OF A LITTLE EXPERT ADVICE
ON THE PURCHASE OF A PIECE OF
property for a new college building. It is to be downtown,
preferably overlooking City Hall, a quiet spot, light on three
sides, and a subway station in the basement, but it will have
to be a parcel that some bank is trying to give away in order
to avoid the expense of collecting the rent. It is only fair that
you should know ahead of time that we Jesuits are old hands
in the real-estate game and preternaturally shrewd.

Our first deal in New York was in 1683, when we picked
up an acre or two for a boys' school where Broadway and
Fulton Street now meet. Our first gridiron became later the
site of Trinity Church. I don't know who the first coach was,
or how much wampum they paid him. The names of the
earliest backfield have not come down to us, but I doubt if

3

they were as musical as they are today. It was a fair location, but we were smart business men as well as educators and realized that land in that part of town would never have any particular value, so we gave it up five years later.

Our next important venture was in 1809, when we were rash enough to buy a farm way out on the Middle Road, in a place called Elgin. The country was pretty and the air was good, but they couldn't fool us! We knew that the city would never move out that far, so we sold the place for $12,000. It is now the site of St. Patrick's Cathedral.

A few years later we bought another farm, this time in Westchester, not far from the Canadian border, in a town called Fordham, because, having analyzed the matter according to the principles of Aristotelian philosophy, we could predict with moral certainty that the neighborhood would always be exclusive, in fact, Irish. With this background, then, of uncanny foresight, I feel very much at home among the nation's leading realtors.

Seriously, though, there is a kind of link between us. Our lives are centered, yours and mine, on two of the main fundamentals of civilization—the right to worship God and the right to possess private property. If you were speaking at Fordham tonight you would probably develop the first, so let me now, with similar motives, examine the relation between your daily grind and civilization, the relation between land and human happiness. For real estate is land, and land is one of the oldest and most tangible forms of private property. It is not only a symbol of stability, but taken the world over, is the principal means whereby a man can provide for himself and his family without injury to others. This touches, of course, the deepest springs of human happiness, of personal success, of social progress, so that, taken in its broadest aspect, as private property you are handling day by day one of the indispensable ingredients of civilization. The Founding Fathers saw that much more clearly than the present generation seems to. Perhaps I am a little out of date in referring to the Constitution of the United States. If you read some of the textbooks on the social sciences used in some of our schools, you will conclude that the Constitution was never meant to be anything but a target for European radicals. But I suspect that there are a few old, doddering, diehards here this evening who feel as I do that, in the wild tides that are surging around Capitol Hill, the old Constitution is now the only anchor left.

With apologies, then, to the Student Union, the Teachers' Union and the Soviet Union, may I remark that this foundation of our liberties, while its chief purpose was not the safeguarding of the right to private property, reveals very clearly the importance of such a right to Society. The authors of the Constitution were, of course, merely passing on what had come down to them from the philosophers of the Middle Ages, and the old philosophers merely analyzed the ideas of natural and unalienable rights. The whole concept of American liberty rested on the fact that God made man for perfect happiness, and so had to give him the necessary means to achieve it; that involved man's physical, intellectual and moral development, and in turn gave him a right to peace and security for himself and for his family, which again in turn presupposed, among other things, the right to private property. And yet today the strongest organized minority in our own country is attacking directly—not so much religion, not so much the American way of life, as the right to private property. On every side we can see a systematic drive to discredit and misrepresent not the individual owners of property, not the abuses that came with the industrial age, but the very right of possession. They do not say "Let taxes be proportional," which is sound government, but "Soak the rich," which is the cry of a mob. They do not say "Protect the interests of small dealers," which is also sound, but "Smash big business," which again is passionate. By constant repetition and innuendo, private property is identified in people's minds with Capitalism—though Capitalism was one of the results of the sixteenth-century upheaval, and the right to private property goes back to the dawn of man. Ironically enough, the attack is made in the name of humanity, the very thing that would disappear from the face of the earth if the attack were completely successful; in the name of that very humanity which is, as a matter of fact, rapidly disappearing in the center of the attacking movement, Soviet Russia.

We don't hear so much about Moscow lately one way or the other. The enemies of our Government have not recovered from the shock of the Nazi pact, and the Government itself would like us, for reasons of state, to forget all the hard things it said at the time of the war on Finland. In fact, it looks as though we are being softened up for an understanding with the most incredible gang of criminals history has ever known.

In the beginning nobody thought that such a fantastic thing as the Soviet could be permanent. Yet, despite the confident prediction that it could not last five years, it has lasted nearly thirty; and is more dangerous now than ever. Millions of human beings have been sacrificed. Justice and beauty and all fine feeling are dead, the land is a spiritual desert—but, judged by its own standards, the revolution has been a success. A whole generation of boys and girls in a community of enormous population has come to maturity, not in simple ignorance of God, but in bitter hatred of Him. A tremendous country of great material wealth has poured its resources into the coffers of a cruel and fanatical sect. Its leaders have made Russia a cancerous growth whose roots have spread into all the nations on its frontiers. Its spies and its dupes now cover the entire globe. A third of the world is poisoned; the rest of the world is sick. Through reaction it has brought about the rise of a dozen white dictators and stands responsible for everything that has happened since. Yet way down deep at the bottom of this horrible convulsion lies an apparently harmless little dogma on private property borrowed from Plato.

Now Plato, of course, was not a Communist, he was merely trying to solve the problem of evil (like all the other philosophers of his time), trying to find out why it was that things had gone wrong a long time before and had been wrong ever since. So he sat down one summer evening in his garden overlooking the Aegean Sea and wove a little romance, which after a while, even in his own mind, hardened into fact.

As in the account of Genesis, he believed that man's first state was a state of innocence. It was a blessed time of contentment and love when men had no need of society. Then the serpent entered in and tempted him to have. For the first time he seized on something as his own, and the possession of private property has been the cause of all the trouble in the world ever since. Civil society, or the State, which was otherwise unnecessary, was created merely to restore the peace broken when men started shouting "mine and thine." And that little romance, strangely enough, is the idea that lies buried under the monument in Red Square. For this assumption about private property—and it is, of course, a mere assumption, a story that Plato told himself in his garden—is the starting point of modern Anarchism, Socialism and Communism. Karl Marx and Engels, grasping at the explanation, added their own embroideries. Civilization, they said, was created by the stronger classes to exploit the weak and protect the loot after it had been taken away from them. So that only when this original sin, this possession of private property, should be blotted out, would all be joy and innocence again. Their more enthusiastic disciples have gone a step further, for they claim that private property can be blotted out only after civilization, which protects it, has been annihilated.

So that all along the line the motif is destruction. In Russia they made a clear division between the "haves" and

"have-nots"—and they liquidated the "haves," unknown
millions of them, in order that only the "have-nots" would
remain. The embarrassing part of it, however, is that the
"have-nots" are constantly becoming the "haves" and the
liquidation has to be continuous. So that, to survive, they
must destroy. In Red Spain, too, when the Russians had the
upper hand, the theme song was—destroy. A few poor, in-
effectual Spanish dreamers, genuine but misled democrats,
thought they could harness the whirlwind with their cloudy
political theories. But the marching ranks of Reds saw their
chance at last to wipe out civilization, so that only "have-
nots," like themselves, would remain. That is why they
sacked the convents and the universities, burned the cathe-
drals and slaughtered the priests by the thousands. Their fury
was vented against the Church more as a symbol of stability
than of superstition or of greed. Though the latter aspects
were played up for a foreign anti-Catholic press, the central
idea was destruction for the sake of destruction. And that is
the idea which, though temporarily disguised, is the central
idea of all the Communist activity in this country; of the activity of the Young Communist League, for example, which
still smolders right here in our New York schools. These
children are taught to destroy discipline, destroy confidence,
destroy order, so that when they grow up they may do their
part in destroying civilization. How far that little thought
has traveled from Plato's garden overlooking the Aegean
Sea! A third of the world is planning destruction of the rest,
because private property has been identified with original
sin.

I realize that what follows does not voice the popular view, but, since policy now seems to demand the appeasement of Russia, since trial balloons are already in the air, the time has come to insist that she is still our principal enemy. Germany is more immediate, more terrible, but less dangerous in the end. For, after all, Germans have been European for fifteen thousand years—Soviet Russia is not European yet. Just now the Germans are highly hysterical, unrecognizable, for reasons that would take an hour to develop. But that has happened to other people, too. England went through a similar delirium in the time of Oliver Cromwell. We may laugh at the people in 1941 who go about shouting "Heil Hitler" at the most unexpected and absurd times, but they are not any funnier than the Englishmen of 1641. The typical Roundhead, for example, would walk into a tavern and take off his hat, bow, and cry "No Popery," whereupon anyone who happened to be sober had to rise and shout "No Popery" in reply. It is true, of course, that even when the Germans are normal, they have their racial faults. You miss in them, for example, the meekness and sweet reasonableness of the Irish! But still, withal, they are people we can talk with, and we who know them anticipate the day when they will wake up and wonder, confusedly, how they ever got that way.

But Russia, gentlemen, presents a different picture. There is nothing left in that unhappy country but a few unscrupulous men with whips and countless herds of dull-witted slaves. They can't think, but their capacity for dumb suffering is infinite. Moreover, their owners can hurl them in such overwhelming numbers against an enemy that their very corpses can impede a successful advance. Thus, Russia presents an appalling problem that will not be solved in our generation, but of this we can be sure—that no monetary gain to the United States is worth the risk and humiliation of trying once more to appease a monster. Let us learn that much from the fate of England and France. For, appeasement or no appeasement, the monster's campaign against us will go quietly on, even after the treaty of peace is signed—his campaign of complete destruction, whose initial skirmishes will always be marked by attacks on the right to private property, to land among other things, to Real Estate!

AN EDUCATIONAL PROGRAM FOR THE UNITED STATES

———◆———

WHEN YOUR GRACIOUS
COMMITTEE SOME WEEKS
AGO INVITED ME TO SPEAK AT THIS
BRILLIANT DINNER TONIGHT, THEY
enriched my education by leaving a number of your descriptive pamphlets with me. These I have read with even more care than a prospective member would, and perhaps with even more appreciation. I read, for instance, that your Charter had been granted by George III, King of Ireland, among other places, and Defender of the Faith. That was interesting, because the establishment of a body such as this upset the otherwise perfect record of that glorious monarch for ineptitude. I was impressed, too, by the firm stand you had taken against the inflation of our currency and by the fact that your walls are adorned with the pictures of so

many *previous* Secretaries of the Treasury. Your regulation excluding lawyers showed a very keen sense of self-preservation, something which is never wholly lacking in a successful banker. But if the reason be correct, that lawyers talk too much, I cannot understand your inviting a clergyman to address you. It must be that you forget the clergyman in the university president, and you know that university presidents have to satisfy so many people that they can never afford to say too much.

It was, however, this very combination of two offices in one that gave such relish to quotations from the report of your special committee on economical and efficient education. It was a thrilling and heartening experience to realize that an old and powerful organization like yours, which in the past has done so much for the welfare of the City and State sees so clearly that commerce cannot be adequately considered apart from human life, that is, apart from human conduct; that even the financial success of our country depends on personal integrity and that personal integrity depends on what you have called so well "a deep, true, religious understanding." Only a very superior, far-sighted body of men would have subscribed to the following sentence, which is perfectly amazing as part of a Chamber of Commerce report and which your Committee asked me to take as the subject of my remarks tonight: "That the United States cannot have or maintain a right system unless it is based on true religious principles and, therefore, in spite of the fact that some hesitate to include religion in our educational program, we place it first."

I only wish that this report had been at hand two years ago, when plans were being rushed for an educational exhibit at the World's Fair. It was proposed to show, at that time, by a series of transparent pictures, that education is a lifelong process to which various factors contribute, even from the cradle. A few of us were surprised to find that religion was not included, even as a passing factor, to be regretted by the more enlightened. But after some debate it was agreed to insert a panel that would illustrate this rather doubtful influence on education. So at the next meeting the compromise sketch on religion was exhibited. It showed an uncertain Gothic arch in the background and, standing in front of it, a non-committal boy and girl raffling off a ham. It was evident, however, that several of the committee members regarded our conviction about religion having a part in education as a curious and somewhat embarrassing survival. And now that I come to think of it, I am inclined to agree with them, because it has survived, thank God, and curiously, too, in view of the unceasing attacks by three generations. The only embarrassing part of it is that our spiritual ignorance lets us down so terribly as a people.

Before trying to fix responsibility for this unfortunate situation we should, perhaps, turn to the recent history of our schools, public and private, because we have in a sense helped our fathers to write it. The public schools were conceived at a time when men had a childish confidence in the wonders to be wrought by the three Rs. Over and over again it was said that, if every child in the country could only be put in a public school, crime would vanish from amongst

us. Today the first part of the dream has been fulfilled.
Today we have the largest and the most expensive public-
school system in the world. We have more students in our
secondary-school grades than all other nations combined.
But crime has not vanished from amongst us.

The report published this week by the Citizens Committee on control of crime in New York is a stirring cry of
alarm. Crime is on the rapid increase and shows no signs of
abatement. One New Yorker in every fifty-three was arrested in the course of the past year—not for parking beside a
hydrant or for leaving the ash cans uncovered, but for serious violations of the law. How many escaped arrest baffles
the imagination. Of those arrested, the majority was young,
resident in the city and far from destitute. A surprising proportion of the thefts, for example, was perpetrated, to quote
the words of the report, "by persons who are not unem-
ployed, who do not live in poverty but in comfortable, even
luxurious homes, who are of superior intelligence." It is
cold comfort even for a native New Yorker to read further
on that the rest of the country is worse than we are. Back
in the age of innocence and bicycles, they used to sing the
song of Eliza Cook, "Better build schoolrooms for the boy
—than cells and gibbets for the man," but now a cynic
might say that every time we put in an order for a classroom,
we have to include an order for two sanitary cells and a chro-
mium gibbet.

These awful facts have been facing our educators for
twenty-five years and they have tried every remedy but the
one you proposed in your report as the "First Point in our

Educational Program." Mr. Owen D. Young's inquiry went
on record as saying that New York State would have its ideal
scholars if there were universal opportunity, a democratic
system, good teachers (who must not, however, mention religion), character building (without, however, stressing religious motives), useful schooling, more adult opportunity,
home rule, with academic freedom (whatever that means)
and finally, economy. Religion does not figure in the report.

In fact the very mention of religion is considered to be
dynamite—as much in education as in politics, for reasons
which were fairly obvious before they were aired yesterday
at the open hearing of the Board of Education. There is, first
of all, the old Church and State row, the old Colonial revolt
against domination by the Church of England. We know
how much validity that has today. We know that the repeated cry for the separation of Church and State is now
little more than a set of brass knuckles for the lowest type
of politician. More serious than that is the view that religion
cannot be mentioned without offense, or even danger, to
certain groups. That too, should be a relic of a time when
people were persecuted for their religious views. Seventy-
five or a hundred years ago, if an Irishman in New York
were asked his religion, he knew it meant the loss of his job
or a fight—usually both.

But I said merely that it should be a relic. Unfortunately,
the spirit of intolerance is still with us, though the sufferers
are now the immigrants of more recent years. That is, I feel,
the reason why so many leaders of a certain group, who are
themselves high-type religious men, oppose the introduc-

tion of religion into the public schools today. They feel that it will emphasize differences and cause discrimination. But that, gentlemen, is the attitude of despair. That is the admission that we can neither make religion work nor educate our children. For any one who is truly religious or truly educated can realize the differences which exist among good men and appreciate the merits of all his neighbors. Catholic, Protestant and Jewish children in the public school can see the differences now, but they would have to think *more* of one another and not less if they knew that each one was proud of his own religion, knew what it was all about, and lived up to its precepts.

The principal difficulty, however, in achieving the first point in your program is the attitude of too many of the teachers. Too many of them have brought to their tasks spiritual ignorance, spiritual confusion, spiritual revolt. Too many have been poisoned by drinking at poisoned wells, and that brings us to some private as well as public institutions of learning.

Like most of our troubles, the situation is a legacy from another generation. For, sixty years ago or more the United States suffered its first attack of Ph.D.-itis. It became the academic fad to go to Germany, just as in a still older day all Englishmen had to make the Grand Tour. There our most promising young men and future leaders drank deep draughts of Immanuel Kant and Paulsen, of Berlin, and found that "the human mind produces its own object, creates its own truth"; that man thinks differently at different times, so that what is true today is false tomorrow. Hence, since objective truth does not exist, who will dare say that anything is nonsense?

From this subjectivism was born the principal fetish of American education—academic freedom. No one has any clear idea what it means. It is mumbo jumbo to anyone who is used to clean-cut distinctions, but doctors' hoods and gold tassels shake with terror all over the country if someone gets up and shouts "academic freedom." So great is this superstitious fear that men have been allowed in the academic world a license which is justly denied in every other. Even their conservative colleagues are like children in a game when somebody has his fingers crossed. For anyone in a cap and gown can blast the presuppositions of life, can rob our sons and daughters of all the principles on which civilization depends—but let him as much as whisper "academic freedom, I've got my fingers crossed," and no professional educator dares to say a word of criticism. Of course, the liberals in the street, who may spell academic with a "k," set up the chant whenever a liberal on the campus wants to attack a policeman or forge a check.

But what about us, who live a common-sense life, who dream a little bit wistfully at times of a world that is fit to live in? We all worship at the shrine of freedom. We would give our lives for it any day, but only after we have defined our terms. Freedom in a civilized country is not immunity from restraint to do *anything*—it is immunity from restraint to do what is right. And that supposes an objective standard. So academic freedom should be freedom from restraint to teach not anything, but to teach what is true—and that supposes some objective standard, too. Subjectivism, however, and superstition, combined with a national contempt for systematic philosophy, have made some of our leading institutions purveyors of elaborate and dangerous nonsense which too many of our teachers have taken seriously.

What, for example, is the prevailing philosophy of education in America today? It is a home product, manufactured right here in New York, but distributed nationally. Perhaps sixty-five per cent of the nation's superintendents of education have been brought up on it. But what are its ingredients? First, Exaggerated Experimentalism, second, Pragmatism, third, Socialism—and of the three the first is easily the most dangerous. For the whole tendency of this particular experimentalism is towards cutting off the past, ignoring the accumulated experience of the human race, starting anew, as if no one had lived before us.

Prudent experiment, of course, can always add to our treasury of knowledge, but scrapping the past can only make us the playthings of intellectual violence. So that, convinced of the old mid-Victorian heresy that man is progressing from slime to perfection and that whatever is, is better than what went before, the men who shape our national education are engaged in a perpetual scramble for novelties. As if we needed novelties! We are nauseated with novelties. What we need are things that are old, things that have stood the test of a hundred generations, things that are immutable.

I'll tell you what we need. We need two virtues in our students which are anathema to the high priests of American education. One is discipline, the other is humility. This discipline should show itself externally in obedience to legitimate authority; internally, not only in trained intellects which can use a set of carefully selected tools, but even more in trained wills. For, as someone has said, "The worst education which teaches self-control is better than the best which teaches everything else and not that." The other essential virtue is humility. This has of course no trace of hypocrisy or timidity about it. It is miles away from an inferiority complex. It is simply an important application of realism. It is a recognition of my own absolute and relative values. It shows me my place in the plan of creation. It shows me my purpose in life. With these virtues cultivated in my youth I can hope some day to be not only learned, but wise. Without them, I can never rise above the organized campus forces of confusion.

Can anything be done, then, in our present circumstances that would further the end which we all feel is the first point in our educational program? Fortunately, yes. The Board of Education took a step forward yesterday, but, as the hostile crowd that packed the hearing gave due notice, the fight is just beginning. We can continue to use our influence to have our children in the public schools—at least those whose parents so desire—trained each in his own religion in a way that will impress the child with its importance. We can insist that schools be not controlled and classes not be taught by professed enemies of all religion, and we can more and more, as occasion offers, lighten the burden of schools, colleges and universities where the ideals that are dear to all of us are still cherished, sometimes at great sacrifice. I cannot be more specific without falling into the role of Cicero *pro domo sua*.

As a matter of fact, all this can, I am sure, be done in stride by an ancient and honorable Chamber which already has to its credit reservoirs and subways, bridges and tubes, the Erie Canal and a report on education which contains this ringing sentence: "The United States cannot have or maintain a right system unless it is based on true religious principles and therefore, in spite of the fact that some hesitate to include religion in our educational program, we place it first."

PEACE
THROUGH
BUSINESS

———◆———

THE HOSTS OF
THIS HISTORIC
CONFERENCE WHICH DECORATES
THE WALDORF TODAY WITH
fifty-two national flags were not interested primarily in
advancing the commerce of the United States—though naturally they will not regret the fact if such has been a second-
ary effect. Their primary object, as reflected in the keynote
speeches of the opening session, was to promote better understanding among all the nations of the world. Of course,
when businessmen invite businessmen to a business session,
everybody expects to come away with a better hat than he
brought with him. That is to be understood even in the
revised rules of the game. Some of the delegates present may
have had an interest in exports which was a little more than

academic. Some may have been promoting the latest type
of one-way loan which is paid off by the mere passage of
time. On a few of the subjects discussed, like private enterprise, there may have been an interesting difference of opinion.

But the serious fact is that, occasional appearances notwithstanding, no group of delegates came to this conference
merely to do business. These are days when every decent
man in the world is fighting to put first things first, to put
himself and his selfish ambitions at least in second place,
especially men like you who have all been enveloped, though
in varying degrees, by the chaos, the heroism and the horror
of war.

Thirteen of the nations you represent have been overrun
by armed forces, starved and bombed and strafed. Eleven of
them have seen their capitals occupied, their leaders humili-
ated. Seven more, like ourselves, while not the scenes of
battle, have poured out their resources and sacrificed the
flower of their youth. Others, whether officially neutral or
technically at war, have been struggling to prevent social
and financial disintegration. So that while you are, I suppose, hard-headed businessmen meeting to talk business,
you are very much more than that. You are family men with
Blue Stars to write to and Gold Stars to remember and wives
who cry when no one can see them. You are citizens with
pride in your native land and love for your people, and a
solemn obligation toward them which you are eager to
acknowledge. You are creatures whose first purpose in life
is to praise, reverence and serve God. And all of these as-

pects of yourselves are heavily underlined by the present crises. So that a civilized businessman of today works harder than ever to promote the primary object of business, to provide, that is, goods and services for those who want them, but now the word service means something more profound to him than it ever meant before. It means everything that will prevent the recurrence of another total war.

Thus, all of you are truly seeking peace in all you do. Some of the less enlightened may be seeking peace for business, subordinating an end to a means, but the noblest and wisest among you are seeking peace through business, realizing the immense power business has always had in public affairs. For even today, in spite of the vast increase in government control which in total war is quite inevitable and which in the devastated nations will be more complete if possible than in our own, the future will depend on economics rather than on politics, and businessmen will have to guide the crucial decisions of our statesmen.

No one, here at least, would regard that as inappropriate. Too many statesmen in the countries some of you represent are retired generals with wives who have no intention of living on a pension; in others, again, too many of them are expansive barristers who have specialized in eloquence. Few of them have ever really earned their livings, fewer still have ever had to meet a payroll, so that when it comes to appropriations—and they are handling your money and mine—most of them have the boundless courage of a simple child. It is, then, clearly the duty of high-minded and capable businessmen to protect their respective countries from the ingenuousness of their respective statesmen. For you alone can grasp and solve some of the most serious obstacles in the path of lasting peace.

Many of the so-called problems that will arise when the shooting is over can be solved without your expert advice. Such things as the prosecution of war criminals—that is, the men who committed fouls on the losing team—and the final decision on the burning question as to who saved which of the allies, can be left to the politicos. They will not ask this time, "Who won the war?" They all know by now that nobody ever does. Other problems will be purely military and it is dangerous to get mixed up in those. Others again will be mainly educational, or sociological, and, though all of these furnish the background for most of the situations that will be properly yours to handle, businessmen cannot be expected to know all the answers in every field. Total reconstruction, which must follow total war, calls for the united effort of every type of expert. It is significant, however, that while all the other serious thinkers are engaged in studying the ultimate causes of conflict, such as empty churches and vicious schools, most of the proximate causes are your responsibility.

If the next war follows the beaten track, it will begin in dangerous rivalries and maneuverings on the part of businessmen; arguments about the allocation and control of raw materials, preferential treatment and exclusive right to foreign markets and difficulties of transportation, especially in the new, unchartered world of the air. To complicate things further at the moment, warehouses all over the world are bursting with government surplus property, war contracts are already being cancelled that will tie up billions in raw materials, more billions are involved in enemy alien property that has to be adjusted. Our holdings in Germany alone come to twelve hundred and ninety million dollars, while permeating every difficulty that arises are the serious inequalities of labor compensation.

Such are the problems that confront you as businessmen. The rest of your responsibility you assume as fathers, citizens and creatures of God, mainly the responsibility for creating good will among men. For every difficulty we have mentioned has been rendered more difficult because of the immense amount of bad will let loose by the inhumanity of the last eight years. Countless millions have had their lives torn up by the roots, and most of them hate somebody on account of it, usually all the people of another nation or race.

Governments, for purposes of their own, have fanned little blazes into conflagrations and, to win a tactical victory without a declaration of war, have blasted with their most powerful propaganda nations with whom they are at peace. Sovereign states have been pilloried for preserving their neutrality, and their leaders and people branded as Bolsheviks by one side and Fascists by the other.

Thoughtless readers in every country have become accustomed to seeing their neighbors pictured in cartoons as beasts and fools and criminals and hate them now with all the fierceness that should be reserved for known evil. There is, in consequence, a world-wide debauch of frightful prejudice that must be reckoned with, not only by businessmen interested in international trade, but by every civilized man who feels that his sense of decency has been outraged.

That was why Mr. Eric Johnston on the first day of your conference at Rye stressed the philosophy of integrity and the golden rule. He knew that as leaders of fifty-two nations and future advisers of fifty-two governments you were seeking first the restoration of good will among all men, not to increase profits alone, but human happiness, too. Let the cynical smile if they like—and they will—at the thought of an international salesman working for anything but an increase of sales. We know that a businessman can have as high ideals as a doctor, and in medicine two motives, profits and service, can and do exist side by side—the nobler motive taking precedence as a natural right. So, too, in business, other things than profit inspire the better sort and while in normal times a great variety of worthy objects can stir a man's ambition, in times of universal wreckage nothing inspires us like the quest for peace.

This peace which you have pledged yourselves to seek is not a negative thing, not a mere cessation of hostilities, but a positive thing, health in the international body, the tranquillity that follows international order. This kind of order, like national order, industrial order or domestic order, presupposes a mutual confidence which cannot be achieved by diplomacy or force of arms. It must grow organically within the different nations: the intellectuals of one nation fraternizing with the intellectuals of another; the workers of one nation understanding the workers of another; the women and children of one nation interested in the women and children of another.

It will take many teachers, many writers, many missionaries working many years, but behind them must be an international business world which does not make a mockery of their idealism; which not only talks about the common good, but honestly considers it of greater importance than profit; which is always ready to foster every agency, intellectual or moral, that tends to increase the respect of one people for another. This is our only hope.

If you were differently minded, and intended to bring back the "dog eat dog" days of the nineteenth century, another war would be on us before we could recover our balance, and all the fine things of life would be gone before your children could take your places: culture, public order, family life, religion. Later—much later—as the wheel of history turned, they might revive again, but your children and perhaps your grandchildren would never know them as we have known them.

Actually, the foundation on which you are building for the future has been frescoed by Frank Brangwyn in the last of four panels on the walls of Rockefeller Center. The first depicts primitive man—"Man laboring painfully with his own hands, living precariously and adventurously with courage, fortitude and the indomitable will to survive." The second shows agricultural man—"Man the creator and master of the tool, strengthening the foundations and multiplying the comforts of his abiding place." The third shows industrial man—"Man the master and servant of the machine, harnessing to his will the forces of the material world, mechanizing labor and adding these to the promise of leisure."

That should finish the story. It brings us up to date, and yet there is another panel left. The fourth and last pictures a hillside touched with sunlight and crowded with all manner of men who have gathered there to hear the Sermon on the Mount. The inscription reads: "Man's ultimate destiny depends not on whether he can learn new lessons or make discoveries and conquests, but on his acceptance of the lesson taught him close upon two thousand years ago."

TO PROFESSIONAL MEN

THE UNIVERSITY IN A BRAVE NEW WORLD

Address to the Delegates Assembled for the Final Ceremony of the Fordham University Centenary Celebration, September 17, 1941

PUBLIC VERSUS PRIVATE SCHOOLS

Address Following the Award of the 1942 Medal of the New York Academy of Public Education, February 26, 1942

THE VANISHING ABSOLUTE

Address at the Annual Dinner of the New York State Bar Association, January 20, 1945

CHRISTIAN HUMANISM AND MONKEY BUSINESS

Address at the Dinner of the New York Zoological Society, January 13, 1942

FIFTY YEARS IN A WOMAN'S PROFESSION

Address at the Final Dinner, Golden Jubilee Celebration St. Vincent's Hospital School of Nursing, September 19, 1942

THE UNIVERSITY IN
A BRAVE NEW
WORLD

———◆———

WHAT WAS SAID AND
DONE ON THE FEAST
OF ST. JOHN THE BAPTIST, 1841,
WHEN A NEW LITTLE COLLEGE

was inaugurated here in the open field, we shall, unfortunately, never know. No program was printed for the occasion. The Reverend Mr. John McCloskey, our first President and afterwards the first American member of the Sacred College of Cardinals, probably drove up from Mott Street, dismounted, stiff and dusty, at the old stone steps, noted the deathly stillness of the country and cried: "The heat is insufferable." At least that is the sort of speech great men really make on great occasions, and this was a great occasion —greater than anyone knew. Everyone hoped, of course, that the new venture would have some considerable success.

Father McCloskey dreamed of a time when there might be two—or even three—hundred students here, and his superior, the young Coadjutor Bishop, was perfectly sure that his college would soon outdistance Georgetown and always be the most important Catholic institution in the country —because, after all, he had not had the pleasure of founding the others.

But still, if some angel of God could have pierced the fog of the future, year after year for a hundred long and crowded years, could have shown them from the back steps of that Old Manor House over there the brilliant and distinguished gathering which honors us today, John Hughes would have cried: "This is Europe! This is Paris! Our vision is looking back, not forward. This is the Paris of the thirteenth century." Imagine his astonishment at seeing you here, a thousand men and women in doctors' gowns, half of you teaching here in this university city, half of you come as delegates from universities, colleges and societies all over the world. How pleased he would have been to see Your Excellencies, Most Reverend Archbishops and Bishops, especially his own successor, the beloved Archbishop of New York. How proud he would have been to know that the Governor of our great State and the Apostolic Delegate were Honorary Doctors of his once little school.

As for us of the centenary year, though quite as gratified as our founder would have been, we are not as much surprised by either your numbers or your splendor. We take for granted, after all these years, the growing spirit of fellowship and understanding amongst educators that has brought felicitations from so many and such great institutions of learning. We take for granted, too, the fact that you have come in your wedding garments—*"in vestitu deaurato circumdati varietate"*—and rejoice especially in this latter fact because it is your splendor rather than your graciousness that opens up the following train of thought.

Here in the United States, side by side with the youthful, bounding spirit of research, we are all aware of a certain nostalgic hoarding of older glories. Prior to the Civil War, this hoarding was rather of substantial things, of educational ideas and traditional curricula. All our American institutions of learning were still within striking distance of the *trivium* and the *quadrivium,* so that every college student in the city of New York knew silver from golden Latin and could recognize the Attic spirit in literature. He was also held responsible for the elements of logic and was never allowed, even in debate, to derive conclusions through an illicit process of the major. On the other hand, academic robes had not appeared as yet on this side of the Atlantic. Old Sir J. J. Thompson, the physicist and Master of Trinity, frequently enjoyed telling us that he had himself witnessed the American premiere of caps and gowns at the opening of the Johns Hopkins University, and used to add good-natured but typically British comment at our expense.

With the rise, however, of a secular and scientific spirit, with the growing predominance of German influence on our leading institutions, extraordinary changes of opinion occurred with regard to the essential subject matter of an education. So that now if one of our first graduates, Bishop

Rosecrans, for example, were to examine the mental content of a modern college student who had majored, let us say, in traffic problems or in hotel management, he might, in his simplicity, mistake an arts man for an apprentice. But as though in compensation for the change of what our forebears would have called essentials, there has been a decided growth of interest in medieval pageantry. Bachelors' gowns are now being worn in the freshman year, in high school and in grammar school. Specially tinted hoods have been devised for the most unexpected branches of learning. Long processions, led by a mace, wind their way across campuses, where not a word of Latin is spoken, to amphitheaters, where not a word of Greek is understood. Schools of Methodology where credits are amassed by future "creditors" are being housed in arched and groined Gothic dreams that would have inspired a Jowett or a Newman.

Cynics may derive what conclusion they will. But to us simpler folk, this wistful glancing backward is a heartening sign. It means that more people than we realize are still aware that education, especially higher education, has a twofold function; that its aim is not only to increase knowledge, but to preserve it; that it must, therefore, always be not only progressive but conservative, in the original meaning of the words *progredi* and *conservare;* that where in isolated cases, familiar to us all, it is merely forging ahead and has lost all contact with the precious past, it must risk a liberal damnation and become (some courage is required to use the awful word) reactionary. It must, that is, double back on its tracks until it can pick up the golden thread once more.

As if to echo this twofold function of increase and preservation, someone endowed this University many years ago with our only endowment, an excellent motto for the official seal: *"Sapientia et Doctrina,"* "Wisdom and Information." The *"Veritas"* on Harvard's seal is simpler and embraces just as much. The *"Yahveh"* of Yale is simpler still and all-embracing. But *"Sapientia et Doctrina"* carries with it a suggestion of analysis and emphasis that makes it a specific thing, a definite educational ideal. For it stresses Wisdom before Information and helps to answer the ageless question: "How much information is it wise for one generation to have?"

Now everyone knows, in a general way, what is meant by Wisdom, even though he may not be able to give the scholastic definition straight from the treatise on the speculative intellectual virtues. He may never have thought of it as a "knowledge of conclusions through first causes," involving as that does, the First Cause of first causes, but he does know that there are thoughtful people here and there who have lived long and unselfishly, who have been through danger and suffering, who have had their little moments of triumph, their hours of disillusionment, their days and nights of silence and spiritual growth. He knows of harassed men who can pause in their incredibly busy lives to say, with the simplicity of children: "I believe that character, not wealth or power or position, is of supreme worth. I believe that love is the greatest thing in the world." He knows that such people have a quality that enables them to realize values, to weigh motives and to understand how God works through His creatures. Although this quality in greater or less degree may sometimes grow in the mind of a self-taught man, or even in the mind of a man who cannot read or write, he knows that there are shortcuts in its acquisition. There is much that a wise and loving father can give to an admiring son. There is much that one generation can hand down to another through that great, deep, wide channel of tradition, the Liberal Arts, especially through the wisdom studies: theology, philosophy, history and literature. For these are the studies that bring us closest to the ideal of knowing conclusions through first causes, of understanding how God works through His creatures.

As with individual man, so with groups of men, whole generations of men. Some we find who lay more store on *Sapientia,* some who find *Doctrina* more important. In the past millennium, for instance, we can discern a kind of water-shed somewhere in the middle of the fifteenth and sixteenth centuries. On one side, the stream of inspiration seems to be flowing from the past. On the other, strangely enough, from the unseen future. The latter of course, appeals to us as obviously preferable, because we are of the nineteenth and twentieth centuries. We have been brought up in an evolutionary atmosphere that leads us to expect, contrary to human experience, always better and better things. We are still hypnotized by the charm of the very latest, the most advanced, convinced as we are that to march forward is always to improve our condition, even though we march from a fertile field into a tractless waste, even though we march straight over a cliff. This modern tendency has of course produced great changes in the lives of men. We are fond of boasting that there has been more progress in the fifty years just passed than in the previous five hundred. But progress toward what? We have undoubtedly been rocketing toward some part of space with terrific and accelerated speed; but when we get there, are we sure that we shall find it worth the journey? We are progressing undeniably; but with every step we grow more conscious of increasing instability.

Even those very ends for which we have sacrificed so much, health, culture and comfort, are being blown from the face of the earth. It is true that killing people off is a more complicated business than it used to be, but are we not cleverly solving all the complications?

When we come, at length, to examine the cause of our unprofitable speed, it seems to lie partly at least in our graceless and unseasonable youthfulness. It may be embarrassing to admit that twenty-four hundred years after the age of Pericles we are suffering from a dangerous and recurrent adolescence, but the sad truth is that when the intellectuals of the last few centuries successfully cut off our past, they cut off, to a great extent, our only source of maturity, wisdom, and condemned us to play the role of brash and ignorant children who despise the yesterdays of which they know so little.

For seeking inspiration from the past is not peculiar to a primitive people, nor does it normally mean that a generation lacks confidence in itself because of small achievement. Rather, it indicates a degree of disillusionment which belongs to years of discretion. Like older men, maturer civilizations have a haunting suspicion that there were heroes before Agamemnon. Rome was in her prime, already showing her wrinkles in fact, when the poet wrote of her the line once at the top of every schoolboy's copybook: *"Moribus antiquis res stat Romana virisque."* And Troy was all but finished when the warning came from Apollo: *"Antiquas exquirite matres."* Greek philosophers and scientists built upon the wisdom of the East. The Romans built upon the Greeks. In the high noon of the Middle Ages, Sentences and Summas organized, enriched and modernized Plato and Aristotle and the early Fathers of the Church. And even in the proud, self-conscious Renaissance, when *Doctrina* began to surge ahead exuberantly, wisdom studies and veneration for tradition were long in dying.

In fact they are not quite dead even now, though Information at the expense of Wisdom has become the earmark of our modern schooling. We realize with concern that too many of our principals and supervisors and university faculties have been false to their high trust. They have become infected with a dangerous—because exaggerated—experimentalism that seeks, like Communism, its real parent, to begin a new world, not by building on, but by obliterating the old. Worse still, the people as a whole, educators, parents and students have yielded little by little to the insidious kind of Pragmatism which applies the yardstick of immediate utility to every subject in the curriculum. As a result, the wisdom subjects are giving way all along the line to the merely informational. Theology went overboard many years ago. Philosophy flourishes in outline form as a species of cultural history. Metaphysics has become a Roman Catholic aberration. Literature, while still conspicuous in the catalogues, has become in practice more and more the science—or the bones—of literature. Of all the wisdom subjects which linger today, waging a losing fight with practicality, history alone seems to hold its ancient place. But even here it is not the more important philosophy of history that is regarded with such favor, but the enormous mass of information which constitutes its material cause.

Largely as a by-product of this worship of utility, we are faced by the problem of overspecialization. The same processes which have met with such success in modern American industry have been applied of late with strange results to the intellectual world. A kind of assembly line has been introduced into our universities, where each of our busy educators, like a factory hand, knows only one operation. One cuts, one fits, one pads, one makes the buttonholes. A dean, a registrar, a department head, a struggling instructor. A strange life that, making intellectual buttonholes for the clothing of the mind! Of course, in education as in industry, the result of our efficiency is a very much cheaper suit. But the method has distinct advantages. It certainly increases the sum total of information in the world and simplifies considerably the staffing of an intellectual factory. It is so much easier to find a thousand brand new, shiny minds that know all about some particular fragment of knowledge than to find one great, mellow mind, broad and deep, the kind of mind that was once regarded as the normal goal of a liberal education, the kind of mind still sought by Christian Humanism as it strives, in the felicitous phrase of the distinguished editor of *Thought,* "to develop the intellect, the conscience and the taste in the light of both reason and Revelation, and with the force of both passion and Grace." There is consequently every sign that *Doctrina* is on the increase. Soon we shall have the universe completely tabulated, and no one will know what it means.

In the midst of our celebration today, therefore, surrounded by distinguished representatives of all that is best in modern thought, we cannot banish the formless fear that this glory of ours is a touch of autumn coloring, reminding us that another winter is at hand. Some pessimistic observers look rather for another ice age that will end our particular cycle of civilization. Would that we could blame some individual tyrant for its approach. Would that we could say: "There is only one enemy to destroy, one 'Rattlesnake' to scotch. If Democracy but attacks him now, with so many supertanks and flying fortresses, vigor will return to our Christian principles. Our Churches will be holy and our homes will be chaste again. There will be respect for marriage vows and love for children. Prosperity, hand in hand with social justice, will enter on the scene and educational institutions will return to educational pursuits." But no one so deludes himself except for political purposes. We all know that the present crop of dictators in the world is a symptom, not a cause. We all know that poor old Europe was already sick unto death long before she decided to end it all with an overdose of modernity. Sometimes we read in

Sunday supplements that we are sinking back again into the Middle Ages. Shades of Canterbury and of Chartres! For years past we have been sinking forward into a thoroughly modern chaos, a scholarly and documented chaos, worthy of our most Liberal and Progressive thinkers. For years past our universities of Europe and America have been hacking away at the twin foundations of their own house. Like men gone mad with pride they have recklessly attacked Christianity and Hellenism as though they could by some legerdemain preserve Western civilization and still destroy the two great traditions on which it rests. For years past wise men have been warning them that if they did not desist from their crazy undermining operations they would bring the roof down on all our heads. Now they have done it. Let us then put the blame exactly where it belongs. This annihilating war of ideas which is closing our hectic chapter of history comes to us straight from the lecture halls of Europe and America. It would have come sooner or later in any event. Our brilliant professors who are long on *Doctrina* and short on *Sapientia* would surely have found some method of destroying us, even though the rulers of the modern world had happily died in their baptismal innocence. As it is, our educators prepared the way for intellectual slavery by giving us, in place of education, bewilderment. In place of Wisdom, and at the expense of the sources of Wisdom, they spread before their students more undigested information than the human race has ever had before; much more than the human race knows how to use at the present time. They produced a glut of facts to which we are not at this time entitled, for no age is entitled to more facts than it has wisdom to assimilate.

Now that the harm is done, however, no one would have us declare a moratorium on information. But as universities our role must be the gradual restoration of Wisdom to the world. We must push forward in every line of modern research with continued and breathless devotion, but, like the athletes in the Athenian races of Pan, let us not run so fast that we put out the light. For the new world that will be born of all this pain must be "a brave new world"—but not brave with the bravery of a dehumanized machine. We want no heroes of the Soviet type to shape our futures for us; reckless heroes who are ready to throw away their lives in defense of indefensible principles which they never understood in the first place. We want the enlightened bravery of Christian Humanism. Our children's children, in this brave new world which we may never see, must realize that they are men, angels as well as animals; men with powers of imagination, reason, will and capacities for unselfishness that verge on the sublime; men whose fathers often reached the heights before them and left inspiring records for them to read, in philosophy, in history and in literature; men who are, above all, God's own children, to whom theology should be an alphabet. Far from despairing then, in the growing darkness, the universities of the world should be inspired by the glorious realization that they were never more needed than today because the Liberal Arts were never more necessary, Wisdom never more precious.

We cherish in our archives a long and affectionate letter from His Holiness Pope Pius XII, gloriously reigning, in which he reminds us that our future is rich in promise because we cherish the priceless inheritance of the past. In urging us to be true to the traditions, the principles, the ideals of Fordham, which are the traditions, principles and ideals of Christian Humanism, he assures us that in doing so we shall not only be serving God and Country, but shall likewise be meriting for ourselves an incorruptible crown which shall be ours for Eternity.

PUBLIC VERSUS PRIVATE SCHOOLS

I AM DEEPLY
GRATEFUL FOR
THE HONOR YOU HAVE DONE
MY UNIVERSITY IN SELECTING
its President for this significant award, an honor which is so
greatly enhanced by the distinguished records of the previous recipients. Its effect on me personally is one of great
pleasure and surprise, not unmixed with embarrassment. I
realize that I should be able by now to hear myself spoken
of as an educator without a twinge of conscience, but I cannot forget the old scholastic principle *"nemo dat quod non
habet,"* "no one gives what he hasn't got." With each year
that passes in the President's office, the business of holding
on to whatever education I once had becomes so increasingly
difficult that in a short time I might be down to the three Rs

—except that I never could do arithmetic. Believe me, however, the memory of this evening will be ever more jealously
guarded in proportion as my illiteracy returns, so that eventually, I shall wear this medal around my neck by day, and
especially by night, when conscience is so wide awake, to
remind me that despite appearances, which might lead people to believe that I am a cross between a business man and
a night club entertainer, I am still an educator in the eyes
of the New York Academy of Public Education.

If, then, your selection had been a merely personal one,
it would have been most kind, if somewhat incongruous. As
the recognition, however, of the part a private institution
plays in public education, it serves to illuminate some very
interesting relationships, relationships too often ignored in
studying the ways and means of preserving our Republic.

To begin with, there has always been an unfortunate
tendency amongst some of us to regard public and private
schools as unfriendly rivals, and sometimes the debate on
their respective merits has reached a point where we are reminded of the action taken in the Oxford Union a few years
back when that august young body felt compelled to pass
a resolution regretting that America had ever been discovered. Public schools have heard themselves denounced
as palaces designed for the taxpayers' ruin, hotbeds of advanced thought and backward results, centers of boondog-
gling and politics. Private schools have heard themselves denounced as money-making enterprises, shrines of obscur-
antism and snobbishness whose only tangible achievement
has been to keep good Americans from understanding one

another. Too few of our fellow citizens seem to realize that, with all their faults, both public and private schools are equally essential to the ideal of American education, that they are, in spite of all the harsh things said, complementary to one another. For each type emphasizes aspects of American life which are only implicit in the other. One emphasizes the necessity of equal opportunity, the other the necessity of individuality. Both have student bodies that are cross sections of the public, both are paid for by the public, both are maintained for the good of the public. Both are, in a sense, public schools, but that sense is analogical, suggesting that an institution can be public in more ways than one.

To establish that tax-supported institutions are of the people, by the people and for the people, requires little logic and less investigation. Any vision of the United States from the Piedmont Plateau westward shows a smiling land dotted from coast to coast with handsome public schools, fairly bursting with vast, eager crowds of American youth. Obviously they are of the people. That they are by the people as well, we used to know from the healthy, democratic grumbling of the taxpayers all around us. Lately, of course, the neighbors have begun to feel that their bill for education is a trifle when they see one flying fortress drop the price of a public school in one minute without hitting anything. But even in normal times, grumbling or no grumbling, it was to our credit that so large a part of our taxes went to public education. The results for the most part were also to our credit. All the grand dreams of a hundred years ago may not have been attained, but that was the fault of Horace Mann and his fellow dreamers for ever imagining that they could be. Crime, it is true, has not vanished because of popular education, and there are at least as many fools amongst us as there were in 1840, but what public schools, lacking religious inspiration, could reasonably be expected to do, they have done. It is to them, more than to any other single agency, that we owe the homogeneity of the United States. They have taken one generation after another from all parts of the world, poured them into the classroom, a wriggling mixture of colors, and have turned them out at the end, Red, White and Blue. Lately and locally, a few of them have been a little weak, perhaps, on the White and Blue, but all in all, we must take off our hats in acknowledgment of an enormous job courageously, and in many ways successfully, done.

This is, however, a twice-told tale, not only to this distinguished audience, but to the country at large. What may be news to some is the fact that the private schools, in their own small way, are also of the people, by the people and for the people. This does not refer, of course, to every institution in the group. There are certain fashionable prep schools lolling around the East whose principal object seems to be the protection of their darlings from the contamination of reality. But these represent a precious exaggeration of the type. Private schools as such run the full gamut from Harvard University to little parochial schools for Indians out in Rosebud, Montana. There are in the group various bases of selectivity, but for the most part there is no distinction made because of color, wealth or social position. Especially is this true in college and university circles where the increase of

scholarship funds has created a new and thoroughly democratic aristocracy, an aristocracy of brains. This means that
our American campus leaders are now a select but typical
cross section of the nation. At Fordham, for example, where
thousands of our boys and girls have come from the public
schools, we are educating a harmonious mixture of Catholics, Protestants and Jews. Last year the President of the Student Council was a Protestant, next year it will be the captain of the football team, while more than one Jewish boy
has won a medal for the religious course which he did not
have to take but had to pay for. There are Indians in the
student body, Negroes, Malays and Chinese, with an occasional Irishman thrown in to run the place, and one or two
Polish boys to make the necessary touchdowns. Thus, private schools are also of the people. In a sense they are by the
people, too, for the people at large contribute at least the
amount of the necessary tax exemption. Most educators realize that in granting tax exemption the city effects an enormous saving for itself, but the fact of the exemption gives
the public a new and deeper interest in private schools. This
train of thought was introduced to prove that private schools
are by the people, but it got a little out of hand and edged
over into the third point, that they are for the people as well.

Their greatest public contribution, however, is not the
financial aid they give the city by taking thousands of expensive students off its hands. It is another contribution all
their own which is of enormous importance, which is essential to the existence of a true Republic. (My fondness for
that word "republic" has increased since the word "democ-

racy" was drained of all significance in the interest of international relations.) A Republic is still a recognizable form of government and still depends for its vigor on the perfect balance of almost opposite qualities. As in the concept of beauty we find unity amid variety, so in a Republic we look for equality amid the necessary inequalities. For in a true Republic citizens are not heads of cattle; they are persons with spiritual functions—powers of reason and powers of choice. These spiritual functions are, as a matter of fact, precisely what make the citizens capable of moral liberty, what give them an inalienable right to that political liberty in the exercise of which they must be absolutely equal. But these are also the very powers that produce certain valuable inequalities, cherished differences which are further increased by untrammeled education. As Felix Schelling has put it: "True education makes for inequality, the inequality of individuality, the inequality of success, the glorious inequality of talent, of genius. For inequality, not mediocrity, individual superiority, not standardization, is the measure of the progress of the world." At the present time most of our public schools enjoy sufficient freedom to cultivate these necessary inequalities, though their immediate dependence on the offices of government is always a cause of some uneasiness. But in the nature of things they cannot, even under favorable conditions, represent all the shades of excellent thought, all the various cultures, all the unofficial and particularly antiofficial attitudes that give a true Republic its color, its flavor, its vitality. Thus, a vibrant country like ours, free and indivisible, must have its public schools, pri-

marily for the unity they give to our scattered population.
And it must have as well its private schools, primarily for the
variety which of their very nature they tend to produce. The
harmonious blending of these two types will give us that
blessed kind of education which in the words of Lord
Brougham "makes a people easy to lead, but difficult to
drive; easy to govern, but impossible to enslave."

Up to the present, however, neither type has been able to
reach the ideal which long ago it set itself. On the one
hand, the public school has been too often swamped beyond
all hope of efficiency. The number of boys and girls accepted is frequently unreasonable—impossible. No principal
should be asked to handle as many students in their early
teens as a whole university staff is required to manage after
they have grown up. Unfortunately, however, in this we are
the victims of an economic crisis. We may boast that ours
is an age of the independent, inquiring spirit, but we know
that it is also an age of regimentation, an age of machinery.
Skilled jobs have increased, but unskilled jobs have almost
disappeared. Thus for a full generation our less talented
youth have been doomed to unemployment even without
the help of the great depression. So to solve the resultant
labor problem, the State has insisted on keeping them
against their will in the long-suffering, tax-supported
schools, where progress had to be simulated by a series of
lateral passes. Under the circumstances, our administrators,
our superintendents, supervisors and principals have been
surprisingly successful, often inspired and heroic. But no
school system in the world can be expected to assimilate an

army of sullen hulks whose only ambition is to be elsewhere. The power generated by resistance to learning is a dangerous force and difficult to direct. Thus the grand ideal of equal opportunity has become in recent years the excuse for cluttering up our classrooms with unfortunate young people who are unwanted in the world of labor, but overdue, and restless to enter it. This situation, of course, has furnished rich soil for certain types of educational experiments which have further confused some of our institutions. For with selectivity gone, old standards in most cases are not long in following. Where formal discipline is impossible, it is only human to make a virtue of necessity and pretend that modern methods have made all control of students undesirable. The root of the matter is that when subsidy comes from without, so does control. The public school needs more independence, so that it can exercise a more reasonable selectivity, but, unfortunately, the man who pays the piper will always want to call the tune, and the musical repertoire of the average politician is notoriously limited. In fact, the only tune he ever calls for is a quaint old Latin chant, much older than the Church, called *Quid pro quo.*

Because of this propensity the private schools face somewhat the same dilemma as the public. Unlike them, we have the power of selection, but we have not sufficient resources to exercise it properly. The old race of benefactors is dying out and soon the great American fortunes will be gone the way of all flesh—and yet we hesitate even in our poverty to ask for public funds. We fear the piper will be told to play his Latin chant at us. Happily, here in the State of New

York, light is beginning to dawn. By an extension of the old system of State scholarships, worthy high-school graduates can now receive substantial grants of cash as prizes for work well done. Thus they are able to meet the increased tuition charges which the difficulties of the times have forced upon the private colleges. This seems to be the safest form of public help devised, a form which even the Federal Government could adopt without seriously threatening our necessary independence. The fact is, some public assistance to private education shows a grasp of changing conditions in the world today. Public control of private education, however, would mark the beginning of the end, for thus all valuable differing points of view would be focussed into one at Washington. With variety gone, choice would go with it and liberty soon after, and without the tradition of the private schools to support them, the public schools would soon find themselves in a strait jacket of the Absolute State, where any education is impossible.

That day of wrath no one expects to see in the United States. Our optimism is too deeply rooted in the spirit of the American School. That spirit is now being carried to every part of the world by the best boys in the whole country. It is teaching them how to march and fly and dive and sail, how to win and how to sacrifice their lives. Sometimes it seems a tragic thing that the best we have are called upon to die, but only the best can ever be trusted with ultimate victory; only the best can be called on for the high ideals that protect the liberty of the Republic from within as well as from without. For that liberty our boys from public and private schools, side by side, are suffering hardships that we can hardly picture to ourselves. The least that we old folks can do is to work together at home in perfect unity, filling the next generation with the same passion for liberty that saved our own, and increasing day by day our mutual respect and admiration.

THE
VANISHING
ABSOLUTE

———◆———

IF I FOLLOW THE
COUNSEL OF ONE OF
MY LEGAL ADVISERS AND TALK
ON *STARE DECISIS* TONIGHT, I
shall feel like a man who rises to give a travelogue on Tibet
or Afghanistan with the full realization that Marco Polo is
in the audience. Whereas (I never say whereas except at a
Bar Association Dinner) in following my own bent and
selecting as my topic "The Vanishing Absolute," it will be
fairly certain that no one but myself will know what I am
trying to say—unless in some mysterious way The Vanishing Absolute gets around in time to the *stare decisis*.

Only a few days ago I was taking dinner at the University
Club. Several who are here tonight must have been there at
the time, because I was completely surrounded, Sir Gerald,

by potential K.C.'s; silk was all over the room. At this dinner we had a distinguished historian who gave an interesting
talk on the approaching peace. He made a comparison between Vienna and Versailles, between 1815 and 1919, and
the comparison ran something like this:

Vienna was a peace made by hard-headed statesmen in
which they erected a very delicate balance of power. Versailles was a peace that could be called an ideological peace,
because, in spite of the fact that here in America we thought
that the French Tiger and the little Father of the Black and
Tans had been the authors of the Versailles peace, the historian contended that it was a Wilsonian peace; that it was
shot through with Wilsonian ideology, self-determination
of nations and all that sort of thing. He went on to point out
that Vienna, with its very delicate balance of power, which
everyone thought a breath could shatter, lasted for one hundred years, while this ideological peace that was founded on
eternal verities began to crack in two years and in twenty
years lay in fragments.

He drew the conclusion that if we are to have a lasting
peace after this war it has to be a peace of hard-headed common sense, arrived at by a group who will check their ideologies in the coatroom. When somebody asked him if it was
possible to check one's ideologies without checking also
one's ideals, he insisted, of course, that it was not only possible but proper, and added that, unless they carry the moral
law in with them, the peace cannot last even two years.

That, of course, is clear up to a certain point, but, as you
know, the moral law can mean many things. Language

among statesmen as among lawyers is not merely an instrument for communicating but for concealing thought. I am sure that Sir Gerald, in traveling around the United States, has found many words that mean something entirely different in his own native land. I have certainly had a similar experience many times in England. Take, for instance, the simple little word "homely." We know what we mean by "homely." But in England a homely person is one who can make a home out of a house. It is very flattering to tell an English girl that she is homely.

So it is with the moral law. Here in this room tonight I could circulate among the tables and ask one judge: "What do you mean by the moral law?" and he would say: "I think it means a more or less constant mode of action that has come down through the generations." In other words, for generations now it has not been *comme il faut* to put one's grandfather out of his pain, and that is why it is immoral to murder the old gentleman. Of course, customs change!

If I asked another: "What do you mean by the moral law?"—he might say: "I regard it as an evolving concept with a constantly changing content." In other words, like the first man, he would sidestep the absolute completely.

If I asked a third—and, of course, in the children's fairy tales the third one is always the one you side with yourself—the third one would certainly say: "The moral law, after all, is a law; it is an ordination of reason promulgated for the common good by one who has authority over those affected, and where those affected belong to all countries in every past generation, in this generation and in the generations to come, only One has such authority. So that this law must be the Law of God. It is the Eternal Law as it exists in Him; it is the Natural Law as it exists in our nature, independent of anything that may be decided in Washington, London, or the Vatican—even independent of Moscow."

It is positive law as it exists freely established by a competent authority and promulgated by some external sign or expression. But even this positive law, as we know, derives all its force of obligation from the natural law according to which certain things are eternally right and others eternally wrong.

This may sound like the outline of a lecture on ethics, but it is our understanding of the moral law. It is the only understanding that makes any sense out of such things as the Magna Carta, the Declaration of Independence, the Bill of Rights—and the embarrassing, partly repudiated and entirely unwritten Atlantic Charter.

Now, this tendency away from the absolute that got us involved in all these definitions is found not only in international affairs. It is a familiar phenomenon to us in education and to you in law. The same lack of absolutes that is making a universal and lasting peace difficult if not impossible, the same lack of absolutes that is undermining the American schools, is also undermining the American courts. Some day I hope a very clever person will write a book comparing our two master underminers. They are two of the most charming, intelligent and thoroughly virtuous characters that we have had in America in the last two generations.

They are two illustrious men for whom their disciples would willingly die: Professor John Dewey and Justice Oliver Wendell Holmes.

We began our legal life as a nation with the conviction that there were inalienable rights that came not from the State but from an eternal source of authority, an absolute, that was superior to us and superior to our State, that could regulate the sovereignty of the State and regulate our liberty; that that moral power had promulgated a law, another absolute, a norm that could test the validity as well as the expediency of State legislation.

It is interesting to note two very different tides that are in motion today in opposite directions. One tide is made up of the peoples and the leaders of the United States of America and the British Commonwealth of Nations. That tide is steadily tending towards the natural moral law. Running counter to it we find a number of our universities, especially those with normal schools and law colleges; we find many of our courts and all of the totalitarian powers verging away from the natural moral law. In all of this latter group we find a common contempt for absolutes and a common enthusiasm for exaggerated experimentalism and pragmatism. Of course, it would be bad enough if our schools of jurisprudence were merely irrational. It would be bad enough if we merely had to deal with behaviorists and experimentalists who consider laws the individual output of the courts, divorced from principles and precedents, and based on a formula which denies the natural law, ignores the common law and the fundamental doctrine of *stare decisis;* theorists who make the judicial process a combination of brain storm, impact of behavior, environmental urge and gastronomical impulse. It would be bad enough if law were merely a glorified merger of emotion, whim and hunch, announced today and changed tomorrow. But we could still take comfort in the fact that such a philosophy of law would not attract a superior type of man. Superior men, however, are very much attracted by pragmatism. That is why pragmatic schools are more dangerous than the others. They produce the same fluctuation, the same uncertainty, but they flatter able men who like to think themselves realistic and self-sufficient. That is why so many of our leading jurists today are legal pragmatists. Does that mean that they are unprincipled men? Well, certainly one who knows as little about the laws of libel as I do would never state as much in public. But I think we can say in all safety that between pragmatism and expediency the difference is a hairline. And expediency is recognized everywhere as the death of principle.

Moreover, the whole tendency of pragmatism is towards social chaos. It is alarming enough to see the *stare decisis* and the common law on their way out in the United States, and to realize they are not as secure in England as they used to be, even though a recent writer in the *Modern Law Review,* an English journal somewhat left of President Roosevelt's fourth administration, described common law as "an immortal old lady, always half asleep, but not quite oblivious, never too torpid to lift an antique eyelid at the slightest symptom of disorder." It is alarming, because attacks on the *stare decisis* and the common law give an ignorant man in the street, like myself, the feeling that there is no certainty in the law and hence no obligation on his part. *"Lex dubia non obligat."*

Moreover, what is to become of that sterner maxim so universally applied by your honors when we poor defendants are dragged before you: *"Ignorantia juris non excusat"*? But certainly, if ignorance of the law is no excuse, what can be charged against us if the law is changing so fast that the court stenographer cannot keep up with it? More disturbing still is the feeling I get that my rights are not permanent any more; they are not inalienable.

Chief Justice Cardozo, in his book of legal essays, *The Growth of the Law,* gave this as a basic aphorism: "Law must be stable and yet it cannot stand still." The United States Supreme Court has been functioning of late under a new formula: "Law must not stand still long enough to become stable." We cannot forget the stinging accusation of Justice Roberts, who said a few months ago that the course of judicial decisions in the Supreme Court in recent years was reminiscent of a railroad excursion ticket: "Good for one day only."

But if the modernist attack on the *stare decisis* and precedents of the common law make me feel that my rights are not permanent any more, their attack on the natural law makes me feel that I have no rights at all, that there is no God, no absolute, no moral law of any kind. It means that all law and all morality are merely man-made, and that is good totalitarian doctrine. It means that, as in Germany and in Soviet Russia today, law and justice are the same thing. Legality is morality, and, in consequence, we have the distressing conflict of law with laws and the dreadful spectacle of petty politicians legislating against human nature. The situation, of course, is critical, but not absolutely hopeless. As we read our history we know that, in the past, disintegration of various kinds has always begun in the minds of an influential group—sometimes a very small influential group. Integration, then, can begin the same way. This tendency can be checked if enough influential people want it earnestly enough to do something about it.

Our international problem may still possibly be saved if the English-speaking world, acting as a unit—and may God grant that we have common sense enough to act as a unit—denying ourselves the luxury of a family quarrel, will go to the peace table with a definite idea of what can and cannot be checked in the coatroom. Obviously, some of our democratic ideology can be checked, can be postponed until another day. It isn't absolutely essential that all the Vassar graduates in Indo-China receive the secret ballot in 1945. Neither is it necessary that Philip Murray establish at once the closed shop in Somaliland or in the Belgian Congo.

If only we can go into the peace conference with one thing clearly in mind, though we may be the only ones at the table who understand what it means, namely, that the United States of America and the British Commonwealth of Nations must defend to the end something far more important than the common law, which has been such a link between us all these years; that we must defend to the end the moral law as it has been understood by our common ancestors for a thousand years. Toward this blessed end some progress can be made if just the men in this room are sincerely convinced that to defend the absolute in our law schools and courtrooms is for a member of the bar the highest form of modern patriotism.

CHRISTIAN HUMANISM AND MONKEY BUSINESS

———◆———

WHEN FORDHAM OPENED
ITS DOORS FOR THE
FIRST TIME—ONE HUNDRED
YEARS AGO LAST SUMMER—THE
only beasts in the neighborhood larger than a fox were the
horses and cows on the Rose Hill farm. No one felt the
need of bears and monkeys at the time, because after all, the
founders were planning a sanctuary for Christian Humanism. Now, however, the University brags about having a
most extraordinary collection of gnus and pandas and boa
constrictors and humming birds. Of course, we graciously
allow the New York Zoological Society to feed and support
them and take credit for them, too, but you will notice that

the Society's official seal still carries the head of a Fordham Ram.

Nor does the partnership stop there. We complement each other in every sense of the term. The presence of so much great nature just outside our gates enriches not only our physical science but our humanism as well, while the spirit of our humanism raises the Zoological Garden infinitely above the level of a side show. Each of us, in his own way, is battling with the most insidious influence of modern times. I do not refer directly to Nazism or to Communism, but to the common father of them both, Materialism, that humiliating disease which has darkened the minds of men for generations, that sinister influence which has sought to stifle all persons so that only individuals may remain. For man's individuality is based on matter and belongs to man because of his animal nature. In so far as he is a mere individual, he is one of a species, like a horse or a dog, part of the crowd, and as such his good is subordinated to the common good of the crowd. But, unlike a horse or a dog, he is also a person, precisely because he has a spiritual soul and for no other reason. He can turn directly to God, possess Him and love Him. So that in so far as he is a person, he is not part of the crowd. His rational, spiritual good can never be subordinated to the crowd. That is why we insist, and always have insisted, that as a person he must be immune from the arbitrary and tyrannical rule of others. For the good of the State his body can be confined—but his soul has to be free.

How essential is this defense of personality, this war on

Materialism, to the program of Christian Humanism is too evident for demonstration. How the New York Zoological Society is any help to Fordham in the matter is not so clear. First, then, we must see the Zoo as a humanist of any age would view it. He would not see it as a child, who often looks in the various cages for resemblances to his mother's friends—or as a scientist, with his habit of measurement and classification—but rather as a philosopher or a poet would, who sees these beasts and birds as part of a breathless pageantry. Each one of them appears before him trailing clouds, not of glory, perhaps, but certainly of wonder; each one of them exerts strange powers of suggestion that can surround him on a Sunday afternoon in the Bronx with green hells and rugged mountains, with valleys bathed in moonlight and endless wastes of snow.

Nature reacting thus on unspoiled man—and any unspoiled man is a humanist—has always made him more a man. Its fascination for him may stem in part from a subconscious yearning for a previous outdoor life, but experience has taught him different and more spiritual values. He knows that nothing orders and puts in proper perspective the difficulties of life like being with nature—unless it be praying without distraction. A personal crisis, which seems tremendous when we find ourselves surrounded only by machines and shallow people, slips usually into its proper place in the general order of things as soon as we stand in the presence of nature, even before we rise, as we usually do, to the thought of God. A quiet river, with green banks, a rabbit, a woodchuck or a deer, can sometimes bring with them the catharsis of emotion that we associate with the greatest tragedy.

Frequently, it is true, the impression is given that nature was discovered by the romantic poets of the late eighteenth and early nineteenth centuries, but what they did was really to awaken a new kind of interest in the great outdoors. Homer, Virgil, Catullus and Dante, to say nothing of Shakespeare and Chaucer, were as romantic as Byron or Keats, and all of them keenly alive to the humanizing influence of nature. We can still hear the echo coming to us freshly from *The Legend of Fair Women* across a space of six long centuries:

> "Save, certeynly, whan that the month of May
> Is comen, and that I here the foules singe,
> And that the floures ginnen for to springe,
> Farewel my book and my devocioun!"

This partnership, however, has been strained to the breaking point at times by a philosophic movement that began in the consciences of men. For, early in the morning of history, about the time that humanists and naturalists began to draw their inspiration from the harmony of sea and sky and open fields, both alike began to study the problem of man's discord and confusion. They found that since the hour of dawn he had been looking for a lost happiness, an inner peace, a peace that can come only with order. We know today from personal experience the conflict which exists between the angel in us and the animal, and we as Christian humanists are still certain that the original solution is the only solution. Our principle of order is conformity to the Will of God. That is the source of our inner peace. We know that this involves self-control. We are reconciled to the fact that this warfare will go on till death and that in this life endurance is often the only victory.

In this solution, familiar to you all, we have always had some naturalists with us, some against us, but never, perhaps, so many of the latter group as we had, say eighty to a hundred years ago. At that time the professors at Fordham were very much concerned about the influence of Compte in philosophy, of Darwin in science, of Spencer in education and of Zola and Balzac in literature. For all of them were working, each in his own way, towards the same conclusion: that nature is the source of all: all is explained by nature, human nature being essentially one with the nature in plants and animals. The conflict in man, they said, was a fiction imposed by tradition. It was man himself who decided that some acts were low and others high. Thus they tried to solve the difficulty of the struggle by ignoring one of the contestants and that the higher nature—a solution which certainly had the virtue of simplicity and apparently other qualities as well that insured its immediate popularity. It appealed to the average fancy as something easily understood which explained everything.

Just as a few years ago psychology was brought to the sidewalk by Sigmund Freud and everybody at the bargain counter became a psychoanalyst—so in the days of our grandfathers another magic formula had its fascination. It did not have to prove anything if only it could reduce everything to a catch phrase that was easy to grasp. "Nature is the source of all; all is explained by nature." Lazy people sighed and said, "Thank God, that's settled! There is nothing else to learn." Then, too, it seemed so optimistic. All we had to do to be happy was to live in tune with nature—you know, rubber plants and rocks and beavers and things! Moreover, it flattered the private judgment and did away with the Ten Commandments. And up to the minute? My dear, it was as modern as stepping into a horse car! In a word, it fitted perfectly the peculiar spirit that was called the New Culture in 1850.

The intervening century, however, has emphasized the inadequacy of such a point of view and now most naturalists have abandoned Naturalism. They admit that it has failed because it shut its eyes to reality. It gave man a picture of nature which man discovered to be false as soon as he tried to live by it. Those few who preferred to be loyal at any cost failed to find harmony, order or inner peace. For either they came to regard themselves as a part of nature, one phenomenon in the midst of a million others, a thing of ghastly irrelevance, or, realizing that they were not one with nature, they felt that they could have no principle of order, once they had given up God. As William James found out— "Sadness lies at the heart of every merely naturalistic philosophy."

No wonder, then, that some of our fathers looked askance at some of yours as they watched them bending over their zoological research. It must have seemed to some of the humanists on our side of Fordham Road that no good could come of what they used to call "dangerous monkey business." They loved nature and the study of nature, but were content to be mere travelers in the jungle—they had no desire to be members of the family.

Now that the smoke has cleared, however, and we can all see beyond the name-calling to definite conclusions—we who have given our lives above all to the study of man—acknowledge with gratitude the help we have received from the great zoologists of the world. For, starting from opposite sides of the wide periphery of speculation, we have come closer together at every step, for we have come closer to the truth, which is its indivisible center. More careful and scientific investigation of the brute has established experimentally what the humanist had always held to be essential—the uniqueness of man. More and more it appears how shallow was the thinking of recent generations when they sneered at man as the lord of creation. They were overwhelmed by the vastness of the heavens on a winter night, not realizing that the arch of one man's brow is more vast than the arch of the sky—for man can comprehend all distances. They were bewildered by the lavish beauty and complexity of the vegetable and animal kingdoms, which seemed to echo everything in human life, not realizing that there is a spark in man, and in man alone, which not only heightens and improves him, but quite transforms the processes he seems to share with wolves and whales and zebras. Now scientists and humanists agree that Rin Tin Tin, the smartest dog in the world, is infinitely inferior to, and is totally different from, the stupidest rational Hobgomadad in the Australian bush. A casual visitor to our Zoological

Garden has only to observe the keeper and the kept to realize the difference between God's footstep and His image, a difference which in this dreadful hour has not only humanistic implications but political as well.

For a new form of government has developed logically from that same old Naturalism which once seemed so harmless and academic. It seeks a new order, new that is, for man, but old as brute creation—the ancient order of the herd. It is the terrifying Absolute State, which recognizes only individuals, which counts its citizens like heads of cattle, which tramples personality and makes zoos out of its universities. This challenge to Christian Humanism and objective science must be met at any cost, unless we want to see the end of everything worth living for. The issue is clear, and in the long drawn out disaster that will mark the end of our great Mechanical Age there will be only one shibboleth, human personality. No matter what the present situation may be, the nations of the world must ultimately be classified not according to their salute or their temporary friendships or their exterior form of government, but merely on this one question: "Are the citizens heads of cattle or sons of God? Are they individuals or persons?"

Only the other day the President of the United States appeared before Congress to report on the state of the Union and gave this striking summary of his speech in the peroration: "We are inspired by a faith which goes back through all the years to the first chapter of the Book of Genesis— 'God created man to His own image'.... Those on the other side are striving to destroy this deep belief and to create a world in their own image." To defeat them physically we need all the tanks and planes and ships which the President enumerated, but for the spiritual conquest, which must follow if we are to win the peace, we need a deeper conception of the dignity of man, who was in the beginning given "dominion over the fishes in the sea and the fowls of the air and the beasts and the whole earth and every creeping creature that moveth upon the earth." We need a society of humanists who are close to nature and naturalists who are close to man, for all will then be closer to the principle of order and to God.

FIFTY YEARS
IN A WOMAN'S
PROFESSION

———◆———

FIFTY YEARS IS NOT
A LONG TIME IN THE
HISTORY OF THE HUDSON RIVER
OR OF THE CATHOLIC CHURCH. IN
1892 a boy and girl taking their Sunday sail on the *Mary
Powell* were blissfully unconscious of the same old Pali-
sades, the same old Storm King, the same old Sugar Loaf.
If they had been to High Mass in St. Patrick's that morning
they saw an Archbishop of New York on his throne, the
gentle Archbishop Corrigan, with a Vicar General sitting
close by (a Fordham man, by the way, later to be known
as Cardinal Farley) and an energetic young rector of the
Cathedral, Father Michael J. Lavelle, celebrating the Mass.
Dr. McGlynn, the newly appointed rector of St. Mary's in
Newburgh, was possibly a deacon of honor. That would

have been in 1892. And yet, these very prelates, one of them dead for forty years, could return to their old places in the sanctuary tomorrow at eleven o'clock and after an admiring inspection of the beautiful new altar feel perfectly at home again—that is, until the time came to walk out into the sunlight. For then they would realize for the first time that, though the Church has not changed, the world that they lived in died with them. For fifty years is a long time in political history, scientific history, educational history, and, above all, in the history of modern women.

Fifty years ago, Pope Leo XIII was in his prime. The broken fences of diplomacy were being mended in Europe and the whole world, for a change, was at peace. Along the banks of the Potomac the air was fresh, bucolic, Republican. It is true that the A.P.A. was getting ready to strike, that Hawaii was about to be coerced into democracy by a band of American jingoes, that the infant labor unions were just beginning to stir and the robber barons were getting bolder than ever with ten fat years ahead of them. Moreover, the Democrats and the panic of 1893 were just around the corner. But for the moment, President Harrison was winding up a colorless and carefree term of office, four years of, shall we say, Coolidge Prosperity. In the social stratosphere the great Mrs. Astor was riding high, reading Bulwer Lytton and thinking about the Riviera, a magic place at that time in a class with Shangri-La. Does all that sound remote? It sounds to me like the War of the Roses. Yet not as remote as the science of fifty years ago.

The greatest difference between that scientific world and

ours might be found in the attitude of the scientists themselves. For in 1892 scientists were sure of everything. They knew that there was no God, no spiritual soul, nothing but matter, which was slowly but certainly progressing by the infallible law of evolution from slime to the superman. They knew that 1892 was more important and brilliant than any previous year in the history of the world because, despite the fact that great art, great music and great literature were going into eclipse, they were beginning to get light from a carbon filament, and tinkly music out of a box. People were joking, in a light way, about a carriage that would go without horses and a ship that would sail in the air, about a magic lantern that would make its pretty figures walk about. In the matter of public health their complacency was equally interesting, in spite of the fact that our hospitals had just emerged from a prolonged infancy of twenty-one centuries; twenty-one centuries of extraordinarily little progress.

The earliest hospital mentioned in history was Irish, and I may be pardoned in the present company for adding "of course." They were always the great ones for thinking up things. It was built in Ulster, when Ulster still had a good reputation, by the Princess Macha of the Golden Hair. She seems to have been a good Irish Catholic three hundred years before Christ and may have had a finger in the following regulations laid down centuries later in the Brehon Law: first, a hospital should be free from debt; second, it should have four doctors (because three might be away at the same time); third, a stream of water should flow through the middle of the floor (the only luxury overlooked in the building of the Spellman Pavilion); and fourth, all dogs, fools and female scolds, with and without thermometers, should be rigidly excluded. In time, this Irish idea of taking some systematic care of the sick spread all through Europe, fostered by the rise of Christianity in the West. Many splendid institutions were opened in the Middle Ages, but right down to the nineteenth century the things that were done for the sick, with the best intentions in the world, were often fantastic when they were not actually brutal. Even the first American hospital, opened in Mexico City a hundred years before the *Mayflower* sailed, was not much improvement on the Princess Macha's, and the same could be said for New York's first venture, a Dutch foundation of 1663. It pains me to remark in the presence of the Archbishop that cultured old Boston did not follow suit for fifty-four years.

By 1892, however, the pace of progress was accelerating every year. The Sisters of Charity, who had established a glorious reputation during the Civil War, were just getting settled in their "elegant" new building on Twelfth Street and living up to their responsibilities as the oldest Catholic hospital on the eastern coast. Their social influence on the city as a whole was, as always, intangible but clearly recognized. Their apologetic value was enormous. No type of institution, perhaps, dissolves more prejudice against the Catholic Church and especially against our religious orders of women than a large, well-run city hospital like yours. Non-Catholic patients, who have been brought up to regard the Church as ignorant and cruel and its nuns as drooping birds in a cage, have been filled with admiration by the cheerful, intelligent, holy women, Sisters and nurses, whom they studied out of the corner of their eye during their convalescence. How many received the gift of faith in St. Vincent's alone will never be recorded, down here at least, though their number is small compared with the thousands of Catholics who have been spiritually strengthened there.

But, a hospital's primary concern, after all, is not with the souls of men. As Dwight of Harvard, the great anatomist, used to say each year at the beginning of classes, "Man is a rational animal made up of body and soul. Our business this year is with his body." So with St. Vincent's, its first business every year is with the bodies of men, but, strangely enough, the word "body" has overtones in a Catholic hospital that are too seldom heard in some public institutions. From the way bodies are sometimes handled and mangled, experimented with and dishonored, one would think that the pagan professors in pagan medical schools were right; that bodies were just a mixture of chemicals animated by an electric charge, and not very expensive chemicals at that. It has been estimated that the sulphur, carbon and water which with traces of other elements and compounds compose the body of a full-grown man are worth about a dollar seventy-five in the open market. It is only in a place like St. Vincent's that the overtones make the same combination of chemicals precious beyond compare. For the body of every old, homeless wreck brought in from under the wheels of a truck, the body of every helpless and unwanted baby, is a tabernacle to a Catholic nurse, a Holy of Holies, a Temple of the Holy Ghost, to be cared for in life as the body of

Christ would be cared for, to be treated with respect in death.

Many of our fellow citizens, of course, have never come close enough to know what gives a hospital like this its inner radiance, but they have recognized for a generation, at least its medical efficiency. So that in 1892 there was little surprise around town when the Sisters of Charity announced that a training school for nurses was about to open. It was the sort of step the public expected St. Vincent's to take, and yet it required vision and some courage, too, to make such a decision. For remember that fifty years ago Columbia's Barnard was just beginning modestly in a private house with many more critics than students. There was not a single Catholic college for women in the world, though many excellent academies and seminaries were perpetuating the gentler arts. Women who had no religious vocation were being trained with great singleness of purpose to get a man and keep him. For some men, a girl needed to paint flowers on china, speak bad French and play "The Melody in F." For others, a knack with corned beef hash was more important. But in any case, it was only when you missed your chance or buried him that any further definite plans were in order. Nurses, for the most part, were still widows or spinsters who had already prepared a large family for death and were supposed to have a sympathetic manner. Many of them were unquestionably faithful, courageous and capable, like the helpers of today who can keep a patient comfortable and get the children ready for school and do the dishes. But the intricacies of modern medicine and surgery with all their various mechanical and chemical tests and therapies called even then for very much more than feminine intuition and domestic experience.

With training schools, therefore, a new era began, and since then every step of advancement in the training of our doctors has been paralleled by the training of our modern nurses. Nurses now have to know their chemistry, their physics, their biology and, if they are really ambitious, they have to so prepare themselves that they will be interesting to an educated patient who is neither susceptible nor delirious. That means in the concrete, literature, history, philosophy and economics. It means usually a college education, and here again St. Vincent's is abreast of the times. Plans are already afoot, with the enthusiastic prompting of our far-sighted Archbishop, that will make it possible for most of the nurses of your Alma Mater to graduate with a college degree, a B.S. in nursing instead of a mere certificate; evidence that they have received not only the finest technical preparation for their work, but a cultural training as well that will enrich their personal lives and add to the stature of all self-supporting women by raising the level of another "woman's profession." It seems a little old-fashioned I suppose, these days, to speak of a "woman's profession," but there is such a thing after all. For the duration, women can be made to do the most incongruously masculine things with some success, the success of surprise such as a dog enjoys when he walks on his hind legs, more success I am sure than mortal men could have in certain women's professions. They can serve as brakemen, and garbage collectors; they can referee prize fights and hold down swivel-chair commissions in Washington. I have it on good authority that next year the Giants and the Dodgers are going to be coeducational. But all this is slightly monstrous and obviously temporary —part of the crisis. The young women of the nation should not forget that nursing is part of a crisis, too, but it is a natural part. Great-souled nurses are going by the thousands into the thick of the fight and remaining always what God intended them to be—women. They are substituting all over the world for the mothers, sisters and sweethearts of America, bending over their boys, making it easier to take, and all the while working as long and as hard at their grueling tasks as any man. Here on the home front, if disaster ever strikes, we shall find that an alarming number of doctors, who understand our ways and speak our language, have been called to the colors, leaving behind a group of refugees, some well-meaning air wardens and the center of all hope, a group of high-minded, intelligent American nurses.

This year, therefore, we appreciate as never before the tremendous contribution of St. Vincent's School of Nursing, but are confident that when peace returns with victory its service will become more valuable year by year, until in 1992 another great Archbishop of New York will raise his hand to bless its centenary.

TO IRISHMEN

THE HEDGEMASTER
*Address at the 153rd Anniversary Dinner of the Society of
the Friendly Sons of St. Patrick, March 17, 1937*

THE WOMEN OF IRELAND
*Address at the 156th Anniversary Dinner of the Society of
the Friendly Sons of St. Patrick, March 16, 1940*

TRUTH IS A FIXED STAR
*Address at the 160th Anniversary Dinner of the Society of
the Friendly Sons of St. Patrick, March 17, 1944*

THE
HEDGE-
MASTER

——◆——

"THE DAY WE CELE-
BRATE" IS THE HOLY
DAY WHEN IRISHMEN ALL OVER
THE WORLD GATHER IN QUIET
exclusive little groups like this, to emphasize the obvious
fact that we are a great body of men. This fact may be more
obvious to us than it is to others, but I am sure there is no
one here who has not felt what a strange and dreadful thing
it would be to wake up some morning and find himself a
foreigner, a Russian or a Senegalese, or a native of Staten
Island.

It is not that we are race-mad, as they are in continental
Europe. I think all of us would admit, at any other time,
that a less favored people might have something to brag
about, too. There were, for example, one or two Saints in

France to match the thousands in Ireland. There was a poet or two in England, though to do them strict justice, it was only English poetry they could write at all. There have been Italians who could sing almost as well as our own, Russians who could dance, Scots who could drink, and Germans who could make the most authentic Irish bulls, but show me a country in all the world that has produced a phenomenon like the hedge school and its ragged master, and I am willing to admit that the Irish are not unique.

Of course, when I select for my special homage tonight the old schoolmasters of Ireland, I derogate in no sense at all from our honored guest, Jim Farley, or any postmaster who ever lived.

If I am naturally partial to schoolmasters, it may be because I am myself a schoolmaster general, but if I am fascinated by what they accomplished so many years ago in Ireland, it is because I am familiar with what passes for education amongst us today.

Way back in 1812, English travelers driving through Roscommon noted with contempt that as they went along they saw many a ditch full of needy scholars. Traveling through our familiar ways today, the same visitors, I think, would see many a splendid school full of natural born ditch-diggers.

If they had gone a step further and asked the old ragged master whether the government was paying him eight or nine hundred pounds a year for his work, he would have laughed at them gaily. "Faith, the government would have nothing for me but a halter. 'Tis the people who pay me—a few potatoes, or a shilling when they have it." But where, then, had this remarkable man his training? Was he trained in a great teachers' college where even the professors did not believe in education, or was he trained in a normal school that would fill his head full of methods for teaching things he knew nothing about? No, he had come back in his rags to Ireland from Salamanca and the University of Paris. He had come back to Ireland to face deportation, in order to keep alight in its little white huts the light of culture. He had come back to be a reproach and shame to the governing classes who gave him his name. For just as it was John Calvin who first thought up the name "Jesuit," so it was the landlords who thought up in contempt the word "hedgemaster." With the passage of years, however, both terms of reproach have taken on a spiritual dignity like the gibbet that became the cross on our steeples.

Now, the name "hedgemaster" calls up a lovely picture of his school, because it was mostly by the flowering thorn on the hillside that the master met his boys. Preferably, he would pick the corner of the field where two hedges met and where the ground was high so that it would give them a far view of government spies, and there—with stones for their desks, and shamrocks for a carpet, and drifting wild Irish clouds overhead—he taught them from his own prodigious memory, and maybe from a tattered book or two. A few little sticks and a piece of turf were kept burning close by so that given the signal of danger they could destroy their poor scraps of paper and take to their heels.

Yet compare what *they* got with the average fruit of a

crop that costs us one hundred and thirty-seven dollars a year per child. When they got through, they could read, they could write, they could figure. That is more than our high-school students can do today. More than that, eighteenth-century travelers were frequently amazed that stableboys could quote their Ovid by heart and that Greek students wandered all over the wild mountains of Kerry. Today we have graduates in Rome, New York, who never heard of Cicero, and other graduates in Troy to whom Helen is only the name of a tennis champion. Out here on Long Island, the parents complain that their boys are being taught baking and moulding with clay, when they cannot even identify Albany. Can you imagine that, Governor? They must have been too young to read the papers when you were up there. There was one boy, though, brighter than the rest—his mother must have been Irish. He said that it was a Dutch town full of poltroons which had been discovered by "Al" Smith. He should have said "who" instead of "which."

If only now we could recapture the spirit of the old hedge school and start all over again! It should be easy enough. It was just a popular system of education paid for by the parents themselves, but it rested on three great foundation stones which I defy you to reproduce now: first, students who were mad to learn, who would rather learn than play; second, parents who were glad to sacrifice themselves, who were glad to go hungry to bed and scrape together three shillings and threepence a quarter that their sons and daughters might enter a beautiful world of the mind and escape from the degradation that had been forced upon them; and

finally, masters who lived for their boys and were willing
to die for them, too.

Was there ever such idealism in all the history of education? Is it any wonder that when the Friendly Sons of St.
Patrick were meeting for the first time in Cape's Tavern
down on Broadway in 1784, a time when seventy per cent
of the English were illiterate—could not, that is, read their
own language—Irishmen were almost all of them educated;
most of them were bilingual—knew their Gaelic as well
as their English—and some of them had Latin and Greek
and French and Spanish besides.

Of course, even then as now there was lofty criticism of
their textbooks—the ones they had or the ones they did
not have—and also of the way they wasted their time. How
could people come to any good end who spent so much time
on song and poetry; when the masters themselves were
known to be the last of the Irish Bards? Ah, can't you see
one of them now, sitting there on his stone along towards
evening, when the sums were done and the algebra put aside
(they probably called it "algeebra," but "algeebra" is closer
to the Arabic anyway). Can't you see that eager ring of
little faces, not too clean perhaps, but looking up at him
with all the clear, fair courage of a great race? Can't you
hear him as he begins one of the old-time songs, about
Granuaille or Kathleen ni Hoolihan, or maybe dark Rosaleen calling for her Sarsfield to come back from overseas
and ransom her?

That was what the landlords called wasting time, because
they did not know that the songs and the poetry were the

heart of the hedge school; that it was the dark Rosaleen who brought those little fellows back, day after day, mad to learn; that it was the dark Rosaleen who kept their parents sacrificing gladly for their education; that it was the dark Rosaleen who kept the master ready to die for his boys.

Besides, after all, what can a great race do when they are chained and bound and crushed by a superior force; what can they do but sing? Historians have praised the aristocrats of the French Revolution because in the filthy dungeons of Paris they never lost their politeness. Yet here was a whole people prostrate for centuries, who never lost their fine urbanity, who never lost their sense of humor, who never lost the poise that comes with conscious superiority, who could laugh and sing and pray and live their own interior lives in perfect independence.

You can joke, if you will, about all the royal families of Ireland, and I know it does seem sometimes as though kings must have sprouted over there like generals in Mexico—though the Gannons, I'll have you know, are descendants of Spanish kings, and they were all great jumpers, too! Joke, if you will, about the royal Irish blood. The land must have been full of it and full of noble souls. For when whole counties were turned into pastureland and the real owners reduced to the physical level of the cattle that grazed on its hills, what did they do? They paid out sixpence a quarter to a dancing master who would go from hovel to hovel with the old blind fiddler, and teach their feet, at least, the ways of freedom.

They were royal in their suffering, our ancestors; they

were better than we are now in the days of our prosperity. And because they were noble they clung to two things. First, they clung to the Mass, which showed them the meaning of their daily crucifixion, and with hardly less tenacity, they clung to the old-time culture, to the fine arts, to the liberal, the humane studies that we are trying so hard to cast aside today.

Oh, if it was the martyrs, the fugitive and exiled priests who kept the soul of Ireland alive, it was the hedgemaster who kept its eyes open, and any real educator will give you one hundred mechanical Ph.D.s tonight for one ragged man who could save the mind of a people!

So our toast for "The Day We Celebrate" is a toast to an unsung Irish hero, the Hedgemaster. May God be his eternal reward.

THE WOMEN
OF IRELAND

———◆———

WHEN ANY FUNCTION
HAS BEEN REPEATED
AS OFTEN AS THIS GLORIOUS DIN-
NER OF YOURS, IT FALLS INTO A
pattern, a kind of ritual. We always have Irish bacon and
kale—one speaker always handles national affairs—Governor Smith always tells us how foolish men look from the
top of the Empire State Building (especially real-estate
men)—and one speaker is always condemned to work on
your emotions and suffuse the whole evening with a touch
of local color.

The color, of course, is no trouble at all. The lights are
green, the flowers are green, the cakes are green, the music
is green, the champagne is green—at least it looked a little
green the third time it came around—and here we have
gathered together all the green bloods of the city, with the

exception of Mayor La Guardia. Senator Wagner has been talking to Bishop Donohue all night in a brogue you could cut with a knife. No, the color is easy enough. It's the emotion that chokes me. For the Friendly Sons have wept at every ancient wrong and laughed at every ancient joke for 156 years flat. The only topic left now that is really new is the "Women of Ireland," God bless them. They are always new. Last year Judge Brogan talked about them in the sweetest speech I ever heard. This year we'll bring them out again, with a little shot of Angostura.

Of course, there may be a few battle-scarred veterans in the balcony who are saying to their neighbors behind their hands: "I wish to high heaven I knew as little about women as he does. 'He jests at scars that never felt a wound.'" I admit there is a point there, but early in my researches I came upon an old Irish proverb, the translation of which goes something like this: "Three kinds of men fail to understand a woman: young men, old men and middle-aged men." That takes in everybody on the dais. It is perfectly true that some of us are happily limited in our empirical knowledge, but after all it is the theory that matters, because the women of Ireland have changed so little in the last few hundred years that history may be a great help to us in solving our problems. Who knows?

Go back, then, to the beginning of the book. The earliest colleen that we read of, aside from the Good Little People who were probably living in the Gap of Dunloe before the old serpent had tasted an apple himself—the first colleen was Caesair, who landed in Galway with her people about six thousand years ago; to be exact, just forty days before the universal flood. They would have been better off if they had stayed in their boats. But in forty days, just by communing with the foggy dew—for there was nobody else in the place—she had absorbed enough Irish wit to remark with her dying breath, as she sank for the third time and the waters closed over her head: "This is certainly going to be an awful lesson to me."

Then the mists roll down from the hilltops and part just here and there through the following centuries to show us Macha of the Golden Hair, Queen of an Ulster that was Irish and free, and Maeve, the warlike Queen of Connaught, and Deirdre of the Hundred Sorrows—all types of Ireland itself. Not many names, perhaps, for so many years; but piecing together fragments of epics and songs from those far-off days, we find a womanhood respected for its purity and intelligence and for its independence too. You will find among the great ones doctors, lawyers and poets and what not. But most of them, even in the early days, were just what they are today, *heads* of families, no matter what the law might have to say about their husbands.

You may think there is something modern in a wisp of an Irish woman who rules her six-foot man with a lift of the eyebrow, but it was just the same before the time of St. Patrick. Even then they hung on to their dowry and their independence and weight for weight could always give a good account of themselves. In fact, they were excused from military service later in the Christian era, only because public maneuvers interfered with their domestic campaigns.

The same sentiment we find recorded centuries later, on a tombstone in Kilmurry, in county Clare:

"This stone was reared by Sarah's lord
Not Sarah's virtues to record
For they're well known to all the town
This stone was raised to keep her down!"

And to this day, a tombstone is the only sure-fire method.

Germany had her warrior maidens, the Valkyrie, but only in the opera house—deep-chested divas with feathers in their tin hats. Herodotus talks about Amazons in Scythia—but everyone knows they were not half as real as leprechaun. Ireland, on the other hand, had women of flesh and blood who could swing a battle-axe with the best of them: Queen Maeve, who could have knocked the British Boadicea well into France; Ineen Dhu, the mother of Red Hugh O'Donnell, who according to the minstrels had the heart of a hero and the soul of a soldier; and Grace O'Malley, the gallant sea captain who sailed up the Thames in her own ship and snapped her fingers under Queen Elizabeth's hooked and painted nose. These were the forebears of the heroic women in Limerick who manned the walls after the breach and died by the thousands.

And yet for all that, the women who fought and sometimes lost were as nothing to the women who never fought and always won. For as Lecky points out so well, "the conquest of Ireland by the Puritan soldiers of Cromwell was nothing to the conquest of these same soldiers by the invincible religion of the Irish women." Who knows but that in this hall tonight there are men whose distant grandfathers were round-headed savages brought over from England to exterminate the Irish race, but who by the grace of God saw the Gospel-light in the eyes of a little colleen and stayed instead in the mountains of Wicklow to father a race of confessors to the faith!

For these women of Ireland were descended not only from warlike queens—they were descendants, too, of the mystical Brigid of the flaming faith. Just as she in her time had tended the Druid fires before the Sacred Oak, until Saint Patrick gave her the Blessed Sacrament instead, so they in their time took their natural virtues—a perfectly natural fearlessness and a perfectly natural strength—and burned them together in a tabernacle lamp.

It may seem strange and incongruous to some who are accustomed to seeing Kathleen ni Hoolihan dressed in her symbolic green with the golden crown on her head, but to me the embodiment of old Ireland has always been one poor Irish laundress whom I knew many years ago—more than forty years ago in Staten Island. Her name was Mrs. Kelly and she took in washing to support her husband and the rest of her children, for her lord and spouse was not quite as much help as her eldest boy Tom, who was ten. In fact, the only work I ever saw the old man do was to nail up a new addition to the house whenever a new little Kelly was expected, and new little Kellys were as good as the robins for telling when spring was due, they were that regular.

I am afraid that some women in the public eye today who have more daughters-in-law than they have sons, and more sons-in-law than they have daughters, would find the Kellys a very badly planned family. A planned family, you know, is one that you plan not to have! Can't our bright ladies think up the grand terms! Planned family! They can make everything seem clean and respectable merely by calling it something it isn't.

The badly planned Kellys, then, lived in a homemade tar-paper shack that was built in a rambling sort of way under an oak tree, down by the waters of the Upper Bay. But inside it was as clean as the heart of the mother that kept it, and the children, down to baby Barney, were all gentle and well-behaved. Even on week days, when they didn't wear much, they still had some of their mother's innate refinement and dignity. And on Sundays when they passed our house in single file, the tallest going first, on the way to St. Peter's Church, there weren't many in the parish who wouldn't be proud to own them. It meant, of course, that Mrs. Kelly had worked far into Saturday night to iron out their shirts and ruffles and press their pants and brush their hats, but it also meant that she kept her head unbowed amid sorrows that would have broken common clay.

She could be merry on occasion, too, and her hospitality was famous among the little ones. Nothing I knew gave quite the thrill that came with stealing down to the shack late in the winter afternoon when Mrs. Kelly was tired after a day at the tubs. She would sit us down on the floor in a row, the neighbors' children as well as her own, and hand out bread and butter with sugar on it. And nothing in the last forty years has tasted half as good. Then she would

light an oil lamp and take down from the shelf the only
frivolous book in the house—*Willie Reilly*. She had a Bible,
but we didn't care for that. We always called for the frivolous book—and she would read to us and we would sit
there in the dusk, charmed by the music of her voice.

Put all that into symbols, and what have you got? *Granuaille!*—the tragic old Ireland that our grandfathers knew,
sitting beside the ruins of her past, with the strings of her
harp all broken, rags on her back and tears on her face, but
a light in her eye, and on her dear, dark head a crown which
meant that her soul was still her own.

Oh, times have changed now. The old Ireland is gone
and a greater, newer Ireland has taken her place—a glorious Ireland, all things considered; one of the few really
civilized nations left on the face of the earth. She still has
her troubles, of course, and will have while English garri-
sons are quartered in the black North. Her leaders are not
as popular as they might be elsewhere, for, being Irish, every
gossoon in the barnyard knows all about running the country, but sometimes I think that her sons are as well off as
we are here and now. Their lives are more like the lives we
led forty years ago before something happened to the United
States. Oh, I don't mean to imply that the land of the free
and the brave was ever entirely above criticism. We always
had a few political problems. It was always possible for a
district leader to exist without visible means of support and
some of them did. In fact, the purloining politician was regarded in the old days as part of the general overhead, like
the boll weevil and the potato bug—and due allowance was

made for him. But when he had stolen the people's money he was satisfied. He never tried to steal their souls. Now there is a new swarm abroad in the land. They call themselves *liberals,* all in a spirit of good clean fun, of course, just as Hitler calls himself a Socialist—being almost as social as he is democratic. So, too, for people who do not agree with them, these liberals are the greatest little slave-drivers in the world. They are not as crude or as simple as the ward-heelers with the big cigars. What they want is not so much our money as our children. They want our schools and colleges. They want the key positions in the civil service. They want control of relief and all the social agencies, and they are getting what they want. Later they hope, when they have the youth of the nation in their power, to eliminate all religion and all morality that does not conform to their peculiar ideology.

But dark as the picture is, it looks as though Western civilization may yet prevail. In the first place, we can always depend on our enemies to overplay their hand. They are too smart for their own good. They are historically greedy and rash.

Our second hope brings us back to the women of Ireland. For I do not think that you and I, mere trailing men as we are, will do very much about the present situation. We are so used to the deadening compromises that a man meets with in the ordinary struggle for existence that we have dulled our powers of indignation. Not so the women. They have a God-given persistence that compensates for physical handicaps. Give the women a clean-up job of any kind and they will see it through to the end. Especially, I may say, the Women of Ireland and their daughters to the third generation. Let them once fully realize that this new and insidious political force that calls itself liberalism is aiming at their school, their Church, their home, their children—and we shall not have to do a thing but applaud their success.

For the women of Irish descent in America have taken prosperity in the main, as Mrs. Kelly would have taken it, had it ever knocked at her tar-paper door. They have remained women of refinement, of dignity, of modesty, of charity, of courage and of beautiful spirituality. They are still a blend of the warlike Maeve and the mystical Brigid. So that as we rise to drink a toast tonight to the Women of Ireland—God bless them! Not only the flowers and the music in the room, but the hope in our hearts is eternally —green.

TRUTH IS A
FIXED STAR

———————

"THE DAY WE CELE-
BRATE"—THAT IS
AGAIN MY TITLE ASSIGNED. BUT
TO SPEAK TO THIS GROUP ON THE
significance of the Seventeenth of March is certainly carrying peat to Kerry. So we always announce the title with
formality and talk about something else. At first I thought
that the Soggarth Aroon would make an appropriate topic,
dear old Father O'Flynn, his umbrella under his arm, shrink-
ing and downtrodden, as Irish pastors always are, humbly
taking his orders from everybody in the parish. But then I
realized how many left feet there are among the Friendly
Sons, to say nothing of the Medes and Elamites and inhabi-
tants of Mesopotamia who are here as guests. To be polite
and bring them all into the picture, we should have to begin by saying that there were once three Soggarth Aroons—
Patrick, Elmer and Irving—who all got along like Kil-

kenny cows, though they didn't play the same kind of bingo. And that, I'm afraid, would call for more delicacy and tact than I possess.

Then it occurred to me that there was some unfinished business about the Kellys of Staten Island, and I hate unfinished business. In that I am like my distinguished friend the great and honorable Harold Ickes, who has taken a private vow that when he leaves office all the business in the country will be finished. So I thought, since so many Friendly Sons have asked me year after year, "How's herself?", meaning Mrs. Kelly, of course, you might want to take up the threads and finish the story, as far as human stories are ever finished.

Poor Mrs. Kelly, God rest her soul, was forty-five when I was five and is dead and gone to her glory these many long years. The last I saw of her was the day herself and all her children, including the old man, were dispossessed from their tar-paper shack by the railroad and passed our house in single file on their way to the promised land in Bergen Point. Her parting words were these: "Gossoon, beware the horn of a bull, the tooth of a dog, the stallion's hoof and the smile of an Englishman." I have thought of her good advice many times since, especially a year ago today in London, when I celebrated the Feast of Feasts in the House of Lords at lunch with the Duke of Norfolk. But I knew that she did not mean the smile of every Englishman at all, but only those too blind to appreciate the peculiar genius of the Irish. So Mrs. Kelly is gone, and the old man, and the family is scattered now; but Mary, the daughter who came be-

tween Barney and Jim, has done very well by herself. In
fact, I met "Marie" the other day. She told me her start in
life had been slow enough. Her first husband was just a
Democrat, but he managed to pick up a crumb here and
there, as a poor man will, and they were able, in time, to
move to the Bronx. Being slightly sensitive about it, they
said that the place was Riverdale. But Jimmie Lyons says
it's as much the Bronx as the Grand Concourse.

Still, Mary was happy up there for years, and when her
husband died he left her well fixed, fixed with eight beautiful children. The last two were twins named Morris and
Sidney, after his favorite Sachems in the Hall. He left
her, besides, a jewel of wisdom straight from the Book of
Kells. "Before you marry again," said he, "take a look at Mr.
Gallup's latest poll on the Presidential candidates." And she
did. It happened to be the year of our Lord nineteen hundred
and forty and the third Olympiad was about to begin. So
she married a Republican and moved into the Fifteenth Assembly District—but she still goes to church. In fact, she
has a pew in St. Vincent Ferrer's, where her boys are learning
from the good Dominican Fathers to serve the wine and
water at the strangest times and shout "Hurrah for the
Jesuits."

Now Mary is the only Kelly I have actually met in recent
years. But she tells me about the rest, and thank God it is the
usual comforting story of the Irish-American, one generation removed. Danny is a Monsignor, Birdie is a school principal, Kate entered the convent but couldn't stay on account
of her health and keeps house for Barney, who never mar-

ried, but owns a slice of Far Rockaway and is grand to the Sisters. Jimmie is a missionary Father and has a colored parish in the South, which the rest of the family has to support. Tim is the poorest of the lot. He's a college professor— and from what I can gather, a great and distinguished scholar of most discriminating views. He is never done shooting holes in Progressive Education. There's one they never mention and I won't mention him either. I don't know what's the matter with him. He may be down in Washington. But one out of seven is a fair enough record. The tragedy of the American home is that too often there's only one, and they would just as soon overlook him.

So that's the story of Mrs. Kelly brought up to date, a story which can be multiplied thousands of times throughout the land. A story of a family keeping close to God, close to truth, keeping close to their own very definite principles. And being a simple Irishman, I have told it with an ulterior motive.

We owe as much to this country, gentlemen, as any other group—and more than some. We love this country as much as any other group, and a great deal more than some that could be named. But we have given as well as taken; we've built as well as shared. When we came to this strange and happier land a hundred years ago, we did not have the Yankee gift for trading, the English gift for compromise or the Scottish gift for rubbing the face off a sixpence. At our worst we were loud, pugnacious and insolent; extravagant, too, and, like the Scotch and the English, too fond of strong liquor entirely. But with these faults went some of the finest

qualities of the human heart, and eternal principles, gentlemen, qualities and principles which the United States needs
most desperately today. Our ancestors were first of all models
of supernatural Faith—simple, direct and complete. They
wanted no splitting of hairs and distinctions without a difference. They had stood up in the face of seven blood-
drenched centuries, and no mere snubbing or petty discrimination by the immigrants who had come before them could
shake their fierce devotion to the truth. When Molly Ma-
guires came around to warn them away from church, they
laughed in their faces. When well-meaning friends suggested that all they needed for success was a little cheese knife
to wear on their coat, they roared with anger. As a result,
of course, some doors were closed in their faces and some
doors are still closed today in the faces of their descendants.
Some doors that for the sake of the country ought to be
open now. For the country needs men who keep faith with
God and faith with other men. Men of conviction. Men who
believe in absolute truth and will suffer for a principle. The
world needs countries made up of such men, countries that
cherish at least the memory of International Law. The world
needs Ireland. And though the statement would be met with
guffaws in many circles here and abroad, the world needs
De Valera. For no matter what else he is—and he has his
faults—he is a man of principle and hence a most conspicuous figure in international affairs. You remember the old
lines from Horace: *"Si fractus illabatur orbis, impavidum
ferient ruinae"*—"Though the world fall about him in ruins,
his head will remain unbowed." When you see him ridiculed

in the press as a stubborn dreamer and an autocrat, remember Mr. Dooley's famous definition of an autocrat. "An autocrat," said Peter Finley Dunne, "is a ruler that does what the people wants and takes the blame for it. A constitutional executive, Hinnissey, is a ruler that does what he damn pleases and blames the people for it." This autocrat of the sovereign state of Eire was told that if he would march his people into war without asking embarrassing questions he could sit afterwards at the peace table "with Ireland's traditional friends." I presume that referred to Haile Selassie and Chiang Kai-shek. But the stubborn autocrat knew his Ireland too well, his own Kathleen ni Hoolihan. For a thousand years she had despised expediency. So that by now she is used to bitter and restricted choices. For generations it was "Hell or Connaught." Now it's war or starvation. She will starve. Maybe she should go to war. Maybe she shouldn't. But depend on it, she will remain to the end, wise in the eyes of the world, or unwise, the last stronghold of principle in international affairs, the mistress of her destiny.

We are Americans, proud of our country, proud of the hundred years of service we have given her, more devoted to her by far than to Ireland or any other country in the world, but thank God we are independent enough to love and admire and cheer for the few rulers left who will sacrifice success to save an essential principle. Thank God we are logical enough to see that we need them, too. For such men are full not only of faith, but of hope as well and charity. They are a lantern shining in the dark to show us the way. For we good Americans all need faith, not only in God, but, while the battle is on, in our leaders as well. After the war they will be held to strict account for every detail of their stewardship, but here and now we don't even bring up Pearl Harbor. We realize that our leaders cannot always publish what they know and explain every move at the time when decisions are made. So we must have faith in them. No matter how things look to us, they may be right. We good Americans need hope, as well, if we are to keep up our courage in the face—not of military defeat, for we are on the winning side—but in the face of a cracked and crumbling civilization. And the dear God knows how much we need Christlike charity if we are ever to see again our passionately loved United States a land of religion and racial harmony, a land of clean, God-fearing and united families; if we are ever to enter again a family of peaceful nations. In short, we need the vision of Eternal Truth—which Ireland has never lost.

> "Castles are sacked in war
>   Chieftains are scattered far
>   Truth is a fixèd star
>   *Eileen aroon!*"

TO NON-IRISHMEN

PURE MOTIVES IN THE FAR EAST
*Address at the Luncheon for United China Relief,
October 15, 1941*

WHAT SOUTH AMERICA CAN DO FOR US
Address at the Dinner Given to President del Rio of Ecuador by the Pan American Society, December 2, 1942

BITTERNESS WITHOUT DESPAIR
Address at the Pulaski Day Dinner of the General Pulaski Memorial Committee, Inc., October 8, 1944

THE MAN WHO PUT FIRST THINGS FIRST
Address at the 56th Annual Lincoln Day Dinner of the National Republican Club, February 12, 1942

PURE MOTIVES IN THE FAR EAST

WHEN THE SHOOTING
IS OVER AT LAST AND
WE HAVE NOTHING TO DO BUT PICK
UP THE PIECES OF A BROKEN HUMAN
race, it will be difficult to determine what blessings, if any,
have come out of the second World War, but at the present
stage at least two suggest themselves for consideration. One
is our new-found interest in South America, which we hope
will outlast the crisis. The other, our genuine appreciation
of the great Republic of China. As far as the State Department is concerned these two developments have had in
them, of course, an element of enlightened self-interest.
That would be true, as well, of many organizations and of
many individuals who are learning Spanish and wearing
Chinese badges for the first time in their lives. Perhaps that

is why we feel so superior at a beautiful function like this. We who have always loved China and see now millions of new enthusiasts joining us feel, to borrow a phrase from the presidential year, like "the original China man." We feel like Mayflower stock visiting Ellis Island, watching boat-loads of European democrats arrive—democrats who are coming over, I am afraid, to vote the Fusion ticket.

My own devotion to China began soon after the Boxer troubles, when the new Chinese Legation was built on Nine-teenth Street, just back of our old house in Washington. All my spare time was spent there, learning Chinese words and trying out Chinese dishes. One night I came home with a complete Chinese suit and a little red button on my hat, and, under the hat, a determination to build a church some-where on the banks of the Yellow River. In that ambition I have been disappointed thus far, but some of my brothers have done pretty well out there. One of them died on the island of Sancian, gazing out over the promised land. An-other, Father Matthew Ricci, lived for years in the Forbid-den City of Peking as mathematician and astronomer to the Emperor Wan Li. That was of course centuries ago, but our enthusiasm has never cooled. There are 850 of my brother Jesuits working in China now and fearing only the order to return. To be very confidential, however, and I hope you will not tell many, my interest in China has always been sharpened by the thought that it was the Ireland of the East. Not that the Chinese are as patient and peaceful and silent and inscrutable as the Irish, but amongst other things, they are the greatest tea drinkers in the world, and students of history can find still more striking resemblances. That is a deep one!

Referring, however, even thus obliquely to Japan, reminds me that we should examine our consciences now to make sure that in the great work of the United China Relief our motives are perfectly pure. It is all right for the State Department to stress the fact that a strong and democratic China is our best protection against the Japanese in the Pacific; that it is, besides, a great potential market for raw materials and machinery. But God forbid that an organization like ours should work to save the starving children of China in order to bolster up a market for powdered milk, or to acquire new bases for navy maneuvers.

Why ruin a glorious work like United China Relief with the contemptible motives of fear and hatred when we can do what we are doing for love? Why think of abstract markets and impersonal armies, when we can keep the real China before our eyes? Start right here on the dais, with His Excellency the Ambassador, keen, suave and charming. Then the Consul General, my good friend, Dr. Yu, than whom a finer gentleman has never been assigned to our city. Go down on the lower East Side and meet the presidents of all the Chinese societies, dignified, friendly, solid citizens. Ask anyone in the Orient the story of Lo Pa Hong, the great philanthropist, or of the talented Chang Shan Tse, both recently lost to the world which sadly needed them. Then read of all the modern bishops and scholars and artists and saints and patriots who are over there now, and finally humble yourselves before the great common people, disciplined, faithful, courageous, crucified. All these are the China of today, and that China must live and keep an honored place in the family of nations, not for the sake of American manufacturers, not for the sake of the American Navy in the Pacific, but for its own sake. So that we, my friends, in the spirit of perfect charity, that contains no hatred of anyone else and no hope of gain for ourselves, must help that China to work out in peace its own high destiny and to glorify God by the triumph of justice.

WHAT SOUTH
AMERICA
CAN DO
FOR US

———◆———

LA REPUBLICA DEL
ECUADOR. THE RE-
PUBLIC OF THE EQUATOR. THE
REPUBLIC WHICH DIVIDES THE
Western World into equal parts. The equalizing Republic
which always serves to remind us, if we are interested in
Latin roots, that a recognition of equality or at least of
equivalence, is the safest basis of Pan-American friendship;
that equanimity is the most desirable frame of mind for men
in power; that equilibrium will always be an important
factor in international policy and, above all, that equity remains in every generation the greatest desideratum in the
sometimes devious conversations of statesmen and diplo-

mats. I say "sometimes" advisedly, for statesmen and diplomats can present a very wide variety of temperaments in a single generation. Some of them live on loftier planes than others. Quito is ten thousand feet above the level of the sea. Some of them succumb more readily than others to a strange disease peculiar to public life. This fatal malady, which is not unknown perhaps in Ecuador, flourishes amongst us here in the United States, where almost every day a public servant passes out with an attack of what we call "acute indiscretion." (We might add, in parentheses, that some illustrious exceptions have made themselves entirely immune by constant exposure.)

With regard to Latin America, however, our indiscretion has not been limited to diplomats and statesmen. In fact, most of the difficulty has been caused by our unofficial ambassadors; by businessmen, for example, who feel that a great continent has been delivered into their hands for exploitation; by professional entertainers, whose style may have been cramped by the police of the United States; by loud-mouthed tourists on a cheap cruise, who regard everything they do not understand as not worth understanding; by professors of the social sciences, who brag about their own spiritual ignorance; and finally, if I may touch lightly on a delicate subject, by certain types of missionaries, well-intentioned and God-fearing men with a lot to learn, who seem to have an irresistable urge to take holy pictures away from little Indians and teach them all about predestination and Pope Alexander VI.

It was this oddly assorted group of North Americans

which found itself very much in the way when the United States awoke to the tremendous importance of Pan Americanism. In fact, with all our talent for public relations, it took us several years to advance from the enlightened self-interest of one administration to the Good Neighbor policy of another, and still longer to convince our neighbors on the south that, in spite of our unofficial ambassadors, we were really sincere in our friendship. The presence of Your Excellency here tonight is a very significant indication that we have advanced. For this the credit belongs principally, perhaps, to President Roosevelt and the intelligent members of the State Department in Washington, but we are glad to acknowledge that without the generous spirit and far-sighted wisdom of Your Excellency and of others equally enlightened, no progress would have been possible.

Merely to mention the bright word "progress" in these days of retrogression is to light a little candle of hope and cheer the hearts of all thoughtful people who are watching the unmistakable signs of a breakup. Forty years ago, everyone was pathetically sure that uninterrupted human progress was the law of nature. We had automobiles instead of buckboards, trains instead of stagecoaches, electric lights instead of gas. Surely men were getting wiser and wiser, better and better. The law of the fang, the standards of the jungle, could never return to our smug little world. In fact, it was rather smart to talk about the Superman toward whom we were evolving with so much confidence. But, now that we are fighting to keep ourselves recognizably human, we begin to see that our progress, instead of being plotted by a steadily ascending curve, is full of ups and downs, crests and troughs, and that at the present moment mankind is nose-diving into one of its troughs. There may have been other times in history when society worked just as hard as now to destroy itself, but never with such extraordinary efficiency. Almost everything that made Europe the center of influence for the United States as well as for Ecuador will be at the bottom of the ocean or blown into bits if this wild scale of destruction lasts much longer. Of course, we are perfectly confident of ultimate victory, rationally confident. Some day we know that three great corpses will be putrifying at our feet. Of that we have no doubt whatever. But we are not too sure that anyone will be able to dispose of them. We are not too sure that these three great nations can disintegrate at our doors without infecting the air we breathe. Here at home, we hope that after the war old industries can be revived and new ones created fast enough to avoid chaos. We hope that our demobilization of war workers and belligerents will be so gradual that all can be absorbed into private life again without too much suffering. We hope that there will be something left of small business and our great middle class. We hope that the United States can keep the production machinery going until all nations are supplied with means of reconstruction. All this we hope, but we are sure of very little beyond the fact that the Axis will be shattered and that, come what may, Pan America will face this uncertain future almost as a unit.

The fact, then, Mr. President, that your friendship in this crisis is one of the few certainties on which we can depend, has taken all the mere formality out of your reception here. This is a friendship of equality that we are offering you, the only kind that lasts. We are conscious for the first time in the history of our relations that we need you as much as you need us. You need our money and our commercial experience. We need many of the things you have, but especially the use of your naval bases and something which you may never have heard mentioned before. We need your South American reverence for the home. That is an incongruous combination, isn't it? Naval bases and reverence for the home. We do need them both, the second more than the first. The Panama Canal may be threatened in the future from without, but the home and the family in the United States are seriously threatened from within at this moment. The situation here is far more grave than anywhere on the far-flung fighting line. For, even after victory has been won, we shall face demoralization in the United States unless we are helped by somebody, somehow; perhaps by the good example of others. Is it too much to expect that South Americans, as they come in ever closer association with us, will preserve what is best in their own culture and carefully appraise our uneven qualities before they begin to imitate them? They will find in us, besides the business acumen and enterprise which they expect, a frankness that is reassuring, together with fundamental honesty and wholesomeness. They will find great charity and much idealism, too. But they will soon discover, if they look beneath the surface, an amazing depth of spiritual confusion and a license that has grown up in the shadow of liberty. They will discover that by 1965, if the present reckless rate of increase obtains, we shall have one divorce for every two marriages in the country, and home life will be a wistful memory. Before that time comes, Mr. President, South America must be ready to show us all over again the fundamentals of domestic society.

Meanwhile, Your Excellency's visit has accomplished a great deal in centering our national attention on your beautiful country. Students all over the United States are reading with enthusiasm about your towering mountains and their eternal snows; your volcanoes, Cotopaxi, with its smoky plume, and sloping Pichincha, with its memories of the great Sucre; they are learning that Ecuador, first of all, on the Western Coast, lighted the torch of liberty, winning its independence before Peru. They are learning also how your predecessor, President Flores, with an unobtrusiveness and a refinement of technique that would bear imitating by the nations of the world today, quietly absorbed the Galapagos when nobody else was looking. Of course he had no trouble with a dangerous plebiscite, since the giant tortoises who formed the only population were as willing to make turtle soup for Ecuador as for Peru and must have been delighted to get rid of the English pirates infesting the islands. I hope that they take to American sailors, as I am sure the hungry sailors will take to them.

Above all, however, Mr. President, our North American students are thrilled to have in their midst the successor of Garcia Moreno. As you know, Mr. Richard Pattee, of our State Department, one of our leading scholars in Latin American history, has just written his inspiring biography under the title, *Gabriel Garcia Moreno y El Ecuador de su Tiempo,* with a preface by your own distinguished Foreign Minister, Julio Tobar Donoso. But even before this appeared, Moreno was a legend in the United States. Second only to Simon Bolivar, outranking Sucre and San Martin, he was among us the best-known hero in South American history. The fact that he was struck down by evil men, as a martyr to eternal principles, forms his own imperishable glory. But the fact that long ago, in the wild confusion of 1861, when North and South America alike were torn by civil wars, and Europe was smoldering with revolution— the fact that Moreno was able to give his countrymen peace, prosperity, education and an honest, God-fearing government for fifteen years—that fact is the glory of the people of Ecuador, a glory that lingers around you now, Mr. President, as the glory of the Republican Lincoln lingers around the Democratic Roosevelt.

Soon you will be returning to your native Guayaquil. There you will be received no doubt with justifiable pride by the university that nourished you and later called you back as professor, dean and rector. Your trip to Quito through the avenue of volcanoes will be a kind of triumph. Your capital among the clouds, with its old world atmosphere of cloister and patio, will welcome you and look to you as its inspiration for many years to come. But we hope that in the midst of your interesting activities you will never forget the poor old Colossus of the North; remember that it will be counting on you for friendship, and especially for good example.

BITTERNESS
WITHOUT
DESPAIR

———————◆———————

"THE DAY WE CELE-
BRATE" IS A TIME-
HONORED TOAST AT THE ANNUAL
DINNER OF THE FRIENDLY SONS
of St. Patrick. In fact, I think that is where Mr. Pater-
acki got the idea. Like many other honorary, synthetic and
annual Irishmen he is always on hand for the green champagne. Senator Wagner of county Cork is usually there too.
And Mayor La Guardia of Blarney Castle with a shamrock
as big as himself; and once in a while, President Roosevelt
who always protests that his Dutch name should not be held
against him because he is Irish "by marriage,"—having
been married on the seventeenth of March. All told, the
Friendly Sons dinner is quite an affair, and the toast, "The
Day We Celebrate," is usually light in tone even when

things are going badly in the old country. That of course is one of the things you have to get used to in Catholic Celts. They can see something quaint in almost any situation. As the old song has it—"Erin a smile and a tear in your eye." In fact, it is proverbial that the best Irish jokes are always kept for the third night of the wake.

Even so, I doubt if you could have found a smile in Ireland the morning after the treachery of Limerick or the massacre of Drogheda, and tonight, my friends, we have news from Poland which for treachery surpasses the broken treaty of Limerick and for savagery outdoes Cromwell's massacre of the women and children in Drogheda. The fall of dear, gallant and trusting Warsaw has been the bitterest blow since September 1, 1939, but the fact that it fell almost on Pulaski Day had a certain grim appropriateness, for Casimir Pulaski, like General Bor whom we salute with homage, was accused in his day of being responsible for an ill-timed revolt and was blamed for the subsequent partition of his native land.

The day we celebrate, then, is not a day for humorous banter. It is a day for deep anxiety, not merely in Poland, not merely here among the outspoken friends of Poland, but in Washington and London as well, where her friends are not quite as outspoken as they might be. For they realize as well as we do what it is that is being destroyed. They know that here is no semi-barbarous Ruritania, or Graustark in the Balkans. This is not the Caucasus or Afghanistan that is being annihilated or sovietized. This is no tropical imitation of a republic organized and governed by corrupt politicians and secret societies. This is Poland, which for a thousand years, ever since the spacious days of Boleslav Chrobry, has been a great center of Western culture. This is the Poland of Copernicus and of Madame Curie, of Chopin and of Paderewski; the inspiration of poets like Mickiewicz and Slowacki, of novelists like Conrad and Sienkiewicz, of heroes like Sobieski, Kosciuszko and Pulaski; the lovely Poland of Helena Modjeska, Matejko, Skarga; a Poland more uniform in language and custom than any other great nation in the world—hostile politicians to the contrary notwithstanding. You could cut off Brittany from France, Catalonia from Spain, and Wales from England with no injustice done to anyone. The lines of demarcation are already there. But when, to appease rapacious neighbors, you divide the smiling plain that stretches from Poznan to Warsaw and down to the early spring flowers of the southern Uplands, you cut an organized body in half which must die or grow together again.

Those who know Poland are confident that it will not die. It has the racial stamina of Egypt, the spiritual stamina of Ireland and the military stamina which we like to consider a characteristic of our own dear boys. The Polish Army itself has modestly estimated that one Pole is a match for sixteen Germans and some shallow people derisively reminded them of it at the end of September, 1939. But the German *blitz* which devastated their country with what was then unprecedented destruction, did not disprove their boast. It may still be true that one Pole is a match for sixteen Germans. The Nazis proved only that the bravest fighters alive on foot or on horse are not a match for a panzer division. They did not and they could not prove that the Poles are not marvelous soldiers. In fact, four years later, after fighting all over Europe, when asked where the fighting had been toughest, these same Nazis answered without hesitation—in Poland.

She had been attacked by the largest army of invasion which had ever been hurled on the first day of a war against an enemy country. She had had twenty-four hours to mobilize. She had no one to help her—no one, and her firepower ratio as against the Germans was one to seventy-two. And yet she exacted nearly two hundred thousand casualties from the invaders and was preparing a long stand in the rugged Carpathians and the marshes, when suddenly she was stabbed in the back by a people with whom she had a non-aggression pact. Her losses were dreadful to read about. Her seamless robe, her sacred soil, was once more torn in two, but her soldiers kept up their fight for freedom on every front in Europe and Africa, the air force, navy and infantry winning laurels everywhere.

They were especially conspicuous in what the *Herald Tribune* described as the longest, bitterest, most costly battle of the Mediterranean campaign, the battle for Monte Cassino, and I think it is significant that General Anders could report later in audience with the Holy Father that 95 per cent of the Poles received Communion the night before the final assault. It is significant because Polish stamina has been linked throughout history with religious devotion. Like the Irish, they are Catholic by deliberate choice. It isn't that they never knew anything else. In the sixteenth century no country in Europe granted more religious freedom than Poland. The Jews found a haven there, and the Protestants were allowed to come and go, preach and teach as they pleased, but the Poles never wavered in their devotion to the religion of their fathers. They knew that the Church had civilized Poland in the first place; that in the confusion of the thirteenth century it was their one centralizing and unifying element; that in the mounting disasters of the seventeenth century—the period most familiar to the American public through Sienkiewicz—when the Cossack rebellion, the Swedish conquest and the Turkish and Tartar invasions came in rapid succession, two great events had saved Poland from destruction: a European League against Sweden and the wave of religious fervor that followed Czestochowa.

So that today, my friends, there is no despair among the Poles. They realize that another league is always possible, though not necessarily directed against Sweden, and above all they realize that God will not wholly abandon a faithful people who for all their faults have never abandoned Him. To reassure themselves that they can rise to new and greater heights it is not necessary to harken back to the tragic days of John Casimir or the disasters that came with the reign of Poniatowski, when it seemed even to her friends that Poland would never lift her head again. They have only to remember their condition twenty-five years ago at the close of the first World War. During seven long years, devastating armies had swept back and forth over the country, scorching the earth; two million homes and barns had been destroyed, practically all the livestock was gone. Her factories were desolate, her finances chaotic, but, most disturbing of all, she hadn't governed herself for one hundred and fifty years and her political sense was supposed to be dead.

What happened? What *would* happen to a great people like the Poles? Brilliant men sprang up from every walk of life. Shrewd Polish peasants, resisting all the blandishments of the Bolsheviks, cast in their lot with the Government. Land was divided, industry recovered, inflation was curbed, an army and navy established and a constitution adopted that for the time and the place was excellent. It would be an exaggeration to say that her democracy always met the highest standards in the world, but under the circumstances it was marvelous that she achieved so much. Compared with her neighbors, she was a model of government by the people.

If, then, she could do such things with no experience after seven years of war, who can say that she cannot do at least as well after only five bloody years with all the great and experienced leaders she now has to draw upon. It is true that she still has her ancient neighbors to reckon with. But will they be as formidable after the war as they are today? I hope not. For if they are, Western Civilization is done for and Poland's lot is no worse than that of the rest of Europe.

Today, then, instead of dwelling on the gloom and sorrow of the last weeks, let us look forward five years to the blessed time when Britain and the United States, having resisted every temptation to quarrel, having settled with candor and honesty all the complicated problems of postwar markets and transportation, will set about supplying Germany and Russia with the things which they will desperately need, under certain just and reasonable conditions. Among these will be of course the permanent inviolability of noble and heroic Poland—*Polonia Restituta.*

THE MAN WHO
PUT FIRST
THINGS FIRST

———◆◆———

NO MATTER WHAT CAP-
TIOUS CRITICS MAY
SAY ABOUT YOUR ORGANIZATION
IN GENERAL, NO ONE CAN CAST
aspersions on the efficiency of your dinner committee. It is
probably the only group of this kind in the city that makes
a serious effort to train its chosen speakers after their ap-
pointment. They sent me two bound volumes which contain
all the speeches delivered at your first forty dinners. You
can imagine their weight. Reading them over (diagonally,
I must confess) I found them a warning and an inspiration.
I was warned to look for nothing new, but to keep in mind
if possible that the dinner is in honor of Abraham Lincoln.
I was inspired by the fact that my illustrious predecessors

were most successful when they quoted the Great Emanci-
pator directly. Even though it was only to retell a funny
story, it was extraordinary how the glow of his words made
the rest of the page seem commonplace.

Unfortunately, there were never enough quotations, for
it used to happen in the old days that speakers had ulterior
motives in coming to your celebration and usually lost no
time in getting down to their mutton. Transitions offer no
difficulty to a man with a purpose—so many of them followed a model of this sort: "When we consider the heroism,
the self-sacrifice and idealism of our martyred leader, we
are brought at once to a consideration of a high protective
tariff, free silver and the unspeakable iniquities of the Democratic Party!" One orator—a clergyman, a Bishop, in fact
—was caught up in a kind of apotheosis. I can see him now,
his face radiant over a white cravat, his eyes rolling devoutly
toward the upper tier of boxes, as he cried: "Gentlemen,
we have nothing to fear. A Sherman in the Senate and Reed
in the House. McKinley in Ohio and God over all!" What
a board of strategy!

It should be added, however, that these quaint sallies into
current history, even on the part of clergymen, were seldom
dull. It was only when the Club was entertaining one of the
long line of compromise candidates who have succeeded Mr.
Lincoln that things sometimes got a little out of hand. What
impresses us most today in looking back over these presidential efforts of the past is the great stimulus that the radio
has been to the ghost writers of the White House. Not that
we can afford to be critical ourselves. The misfortune of our

Chief Executives speaking at this dinner was that of any speaker who has to mingle his own rhythms with the scriptural prose of Lincoln; of any thinker who has to stand comparison with a completely honest and lucid mind; of any politician who has to measure up to a man who always put first things first. Their misfortune was that, with the single exception of Theodore Roosevelt, they did not "belong to the ages." Like most of us here tonight, they were men of the hour, sometimes pathetically topical, all wrapped in "little hot cold violent affected brand new habits of mind" that can look like the real thing sometimes for five or ten years, and all the while, looming behind them, stood one of the few great characters of history. He said himself one time: "I have talked with many great men and I do not see how they differ from others." What he meant, of course, was that he had talked with men who were considered great by their contemporaries. It is entirely possible that even with five years in Washington he never met a really great man, certain that he never met a man as great as himself. For there was no one around him who blended so perfectly the spirit of his time with eternal principles.

To say, therefore, that Lincoln was a real mid-nineteenth-century American, detracts in no way from his greatness. In the same way, Dante was a thirteenth-century Florentine and Homer a primitive Greek. His stovepipe hat, his chin whiskers and his boots were just what we can see in our own family album. He never pressed his pants, but neither did any of the generals with whom he had so many pictures taken. Inside, too, he was one of our grandfathers. There

was even something of the backwoodsman about him right
to the end. Much of his horse sense and many of his jokes
were full of nineteenth-century tobacco juice. We wonder,
sometimes, what the powdered wigs at Mount Vernon would
have thought of him and can imagine what consternation
he would cause on Pennsylvania Avenue today. In fact, it
is hard to picture him just as he was except in the horsehair
trimmings of 1860—and yet he rose so triumphantly above
his generation.

Small minds, then as now, could not tell means from
ends. Politicians, then as now, were taking their cue from
popular passions, their only principle being that leaders of
the people must always follow them. Everyone in the Northern States knew that their need was greater than ever before
and prayed for a man who would be equal to this crisis. But
when Abraham Lincoln was given to them, the great ones
of the world could not see higher than his bootstraps. To
Samuel Bowles, of the *Springfield Republican,* Lincoln was
"a simple susan;" to Governor Andrews, of Massachusetts,
he was "a rowdy;" to Wendell Phillips, he was a "tortoise"
and a "slave hound"—while from Brooklyn came the wail
of Henry Ward Beecher: "Never was a time when men's
prayers so fervently asked God for a leader. He has refused
our petition. Not a spark of genius has Lincoln, not an element of leadership!"

As so often happens, it took the common people to sense
true greatness. During one of his receptions, a man of no
consequence, a typical American, approached him and said:
"Mr. Lincoln, I have watched you closely ever since your

inauguration. As one of your constituents I now say to you, do in the future as you damn please and I will support you." "Sit down, my friend," said the President, "I haven't seen half enough of you." What was the secret? What did the people instinctively sense as they "watched him closely"? His single-mindedness. The invariable habit of putting first things first. They saw that he had one ultimate purpose in public life and that was the liberty of his country. Everything else was a means to that end, including his own political career. They had seen him time and again stand out against the passions of the electorate and do the unpopular thing. As a newcomer in the House of Representatives, he found that the people were being whipped up to a war against Mexico on a fake issue. Older and smarter men told him to lie low. His answer was the Spot Resolution. Shortly after, the "Know Nothings," wrapped up in the Stars and Stripes, set out to prove what good Americans its members were by burning churches and schools and stoning naturalized citizens in the streets. We blush today to think how popular the movement was, but actually it spread like wildfire, so that for a while the clever way to win an election was to curry favor with these gallant sons of the Bill of Rights. Lincoln, who needed the votes as much as anyone, openly declared that if they succeeded in their program, "he hoped that he might live in Russia, where he could take his despotism pure and simple without the base alloy of hyprocrisy."

Later still, when he began to emerge as a presidential possibility, the smart boys urged him to stay on the fence so as not to arouse the South. He replied with his famous speech on the house divided against itself. And so it was to the end. Had he lived another twenty-four hours, he would have made another unpopular speech. For on the 15th of April, 1865, he was to have held a reception for the new British Minister, Sir Frederic Bruce. The shooting took place on the night of the 14th, and early the next morning he was dead. Everyone knew, most of all Lincoln, what England had done to embarrass the Federal Government during the Civil War. Everyone knew that the Confederate navy had been built in British shipyards, that the blockade runners of the South which kept the Confederacy alive could have done so only with the co-operation of the British West Indies. Everyone had read Gladstone's speech as Chancellor of the Exchequer, exulting in the House of Commons because Jeff Davis "had created a new nation." Everyone knew that, though the millhands of Lancashire and a few great men like John Bright, Richard Cobden and the Prince Consort were our friends, the old school ties were all against us —and resentment in America was still very deep. Lincoln's own feelings were doubtless the feelings of the people, but the gratification of his feelings was never the purpose of his life. That purpose was the liberty of his country, and it was common sense that that liberty would be further assured by the friendship of Great Britain, which at that time had reached her apogee. This, then, was the heart of the drafted speech intended for the British Minister and found among Lincoln's papers after his death: "The interest of civilization and humanity require that the two should be friends. I have always known and accepted it as a fact that the Queen of England is a sincere and honest well-wisher of the United States. I have been equally frank and explicit in the opinion that the friendship of the United States toward Great Britain is enjoined by all the considerations of interest and of sentiment affecting the character of both."

A similar situation is bound to appear after the surrender of Germany. Someone will have to rise above the passions of the rest of us. Someone will have to see that the accidental alignment of nations in any single conflict cannot forever affect their friendships or their enmities. There is a bigger plan for the peoples of the world than any little group of statesmen can create and there are fundamental differences of principle involved which all the dossiers of diplomacy cannot obscure. Whoever is to unravel our tangled skein after victory has been won must be able in his public and his private life to compare every movement, every step, with one main purpose, as Lincoln did. With Lincoln it was the liberty of his country. If he could have had liberty without Union, he might have let Union go. If he could have had liberty without emancipation, he might have let emancipation go; if he could have had liberty without war, he would have been the happiest man alive. But liberty he had to have.

Such was his singleness of purpose. Where did he get the strength to see it through? If you want to find out by indirection, read one of poor Bob Ingersoll's Lincoln speeches and determine for yourselves why it rings like a tin can. You will see at once that it is because the eloquent atheist, the spellbinder who dethroned Almighty God forever—about fifty years ago—wanted to avoid the central fact of

Lincoln's character. It embarrassed him that a man who was neither a clerical hypocrite nor an ignorant farmer could say, for example, at Lancaster, Pennsylvania: "You all may recollect that in taking up the sword thus forced into our hands, this Government appealed to the prayers of the pious and the good, and declared that it placed its whole dependence upon the favor of God. I now humbly and reverently in your presence reiterate the acknowledgment of that dependence, not doubting that, if it shall please the Divine Being who determines the destinies of nations, this shall remain a united people; they will, humbly seeking the Divine guidance, make their prolonged national existence a source of new benefits to themselves and their successors, and to all classes and conditions of mankind." Or again, in speaking to the old-school Presbyterians of Baltimore: "I was early brought to a lively reflection that nothing in my power, or others, to rely upon would succeed without direct assistance from the Almighty. I have often wished that I was a more devout man than I am. Nevertheless, amid the greatest difficulties of my administration, when I could not see any other resort, I would place my whole reliance in God, knowing that He would decide for the right."

Imagine the discomfort of Colonel Ingersoll and the other materialistic atheists, the philosophical Nazis who have thought the world into its present state of civilization, as they read of Lincoln locked in his room during the battle of Gettysburg, down on his knees, his great head in his hands, praying like a child. "I told God that I had done all that I could and that now the result was in His hands; that if this country was to be saved, it was because He so willed it! The burden rolled off my shoulders. My intense anxiety was relieved and in its place came a great trustfulness!" Poor old Ingersoll! To make a Lincoln Day address, logic should have driven him to say, "He was a great man, but the source of all his strength was superstition!"

Tonight once more we stand at the crossroads. Like Lincoln and his followers, we are fighting for a cosmic concept: personal freedom with all its many implications the world over. In 1860 the democratic experiment that America had so triumphantly launched in the War of Independence was hanging in the balance. If our way of living perished in America, it would perish everywhere. And what was this way of living? In its simplest terms it was a recognition of the dignity of man as a person. Personality, not "sociality," was the foundation of our Republic, and a person differs from a wolf in the pack in this alone, that he can think and choose—activities that rise above the power of matter. Thus, our way of life is bound up with a recognition of the spiritual soul, and the first expression of American liberty begins with the reverent acknowledgment of God as its source.

What the country needed in 1860, it must have today. Leaders with a single purpose, and a great reserve of spiritual strength; people who know that they are fighting in a just cause, and who in a new, clear vision born of suffering will abandon the smart-aleck gods of the last fifty years and recognize that their Creator, their souls and their liberties are inseparably bound together. All this they can read in their Bible; they can read it more scientifically expressed in

St. Thomas Aquinas and St. Robert Bellarmine—but, if they can read the lines of a human face, they can read it all in the face of Abraham Lincoln.

TO FELLOWMEN

TOLERANCE OR CHARITY
Address at the Annual Dinner of the Committee of the Conference of Jews and Christians, Boston Chamber of Commerce, April 23, 1942

LUCIFER ATTITUDINIZING
Address on the Columbia Broadcasting System Symposium on the Persecution in Germany, November 14, 1938

ART AND TRADITION
Address at the Luncheon Launching the Subscription Campaign, Metropolitan Museum of Art, January 20, 1946

THE JESUIT ENIGMA
Address at the Annual Communion Breakfast of the Sons of Xavier, March 10, 1940

LABOR AND THE PRIESTHOOD
Address at the Testimonial Dinner for the Reverend John P. Boland, New York State Labor Relations Board, December 9, 1942

HOPE AND RED HATS
Address at the Charter Centenary Dinner of Fordham University, May 11, 1946

TOLERANCE

OR CHARITY

❦

THE SPIRIT OF THIS
MEETING HAS BEEN EX-
EMPLIFIED VERY DRAMATICALLY IN
THE SELECTION OF AT LEAST ONE
name on the program. There was a time, I am sure, when
Mr. Adams' ancestors would have thought twice before
sending to the dockyards of America for a speaker. Can't
you imagine the comment in the early pages of the *Boston
Transcript*—"New York, indeed! Since when has Athens
had to go to Boeotia for anything?" Of course, we still cherish the story of the customer who wrote to the Boston book-
seller ordering a copy of Canon Farrar's *Seekers After God*,
only to receive the following telegram: "No seekers after
God in Boston. Try New York." The fact that the present
speaker is not only a New Yorker with all the handicaps
implied, but a Roman Catholic priest, a notorious Irishman
and—shades of Cotton Mather—a Jesuit as well, is clear

proof that your chairman has thrown discretion to the wind in his pursuit of an ideal.

That ideal, however, is not, I hope, the ideal of mere tolerance. For tolerance, it should be said at once, is the lowest form of human co-operation. It is the drab, uncomfortable, halfway house between hate and charity. I should never have come here tonight just to be tolerated by all these agreeable Jews and Protestants. I came because I was convinced that they have a positive interest in me, as I have in them. To be tolerated is to be put in a class with hay fever. It means that other people can put up with you, bear you, to go back to the original sense of the word; but who wants to be put up with? It is humiliating to be tolerated socially—and being tolerated in intellectual and spiritual spheres is a very complicated business, so complicated that I hardly know exactly how it is done.

For any man who believes in objective truth, as I do, who believes that it is possible to be sure of some things, as I most certainly do, knows that every fact of which he becomes certain limits the extent of his tolerance for other people's ideas and opinions. Once I am convinced that two times two equals four, my tolerance on that point is at an end. I can tolerate, I can even love a dear old lady who has learned in the cult of the Mystical Oom that two times two equals five, but I cannot be tolerant toward what I know to be a mental aberration. Sometimes, of course, we can humor a child, or a friend, or a drunk, and politely pretend a tolerance we do not actually feel—as we do in New York when nice people from Brooklyn start talking about the

Dodgers. We act the part of Polonius, trying to prevent Hamlet from becoming violent. "By the Mass, and 'tis like a camel, indeed. It is backed like a weasel, aye, very like a whale." But yesterday I had a letter from "The Euthanasia Society of America, Incorporated," seeking tolerance of their views on murder and suicide. The argument seems to be that if you can chloroform a pet cat because it has a broken leg, the State should not prevent you from using the same benevolent discretion on your wife. What tolerance can any sane American have for that view or the argument used to back it up? If they had said "Two million American mothers every year murder their own babies and the State doesn't make much fuss about it because the babies are not pretty yet; why shouldn't the same women be allowed to murder their old fathers since they are not pretty any more?"—that would be an argument I could tolerate because it does establish at least the inconsistency of the State; but I would still refuse to tolerate the suppositions of the argument and would still insist that the deluded sentimentalists, who are bringing pressure to bear on a confused public, are a social menace and should be treated as such.

What, then, about religious differences of opinion? If mere opinion is involved, tolerance is easy for educated people. But if it is a matter of affirming, on the one hand, and denying, on the other, the existence of a fact, no intellectual tolerance is possible. When a beautiful character, a model of charity, and my best friend says to me in all seriousness: "You are sure that Christ was divine. I am sure He was not, but we can tolerate each other's conclusions"—I know that he has studied his philosophy in some institution where they do not include logic in the course. We can tolerate each other. We can love each other, but we cannot tolerate each other's contradictory conclusions without intellectual chaos; without falling into that strangest of modern errors, "One religion is as good as another." What most people mean to say when they use that familiar tag is that it is a good thing for everybody to believe at least in the existence of God. One of our old Fathers, on parlor duty in the Rectory, was being plagued one time by a society woman who had what she called intellectual difficulties about everything in general. Finally he interrupted her long enough to say: "But you do believe in the principle of contradiction? Yes? Well, hang on to that and try to live up to it!" Personally, if I ever became convinced that one religion was as good as another, I should become an absolute agnostic. I am perfectly sure of my position, and yet for those who disagree with me, I have a great deal more than toleration. I have at least a feeling of civic friendship, and that for several reasons.

To begin with the most remote and sentimental, we are, when all is said and done, members of the same family— not merely we—Protestants, Jews and Catholics gathered here in Boston for this lovely dinner—but all the men and women who ever lived, for we are descended from the same unhappy parents. Vestiges of a common language persist in the most widely scattered races. It is a touching thing that fragments of our primitive tongue seem to express the dearest things in life—*bera, bhratar, frater, brodir, bruder, brother;* and *pidar, pitar, pater, fader, father.* In that, we are all, after a fashion, co-linguals, but it doesn't seem to mean much, even where the languages are very close. Look at China and Japan, Poland and Russia, Italy and France, Germany and England. Even here in the melting pot of the United States a bond is necessary, much stronger than anything ethnology can offer. For language and prehistoric ancestry are after all remote and academic things. Why should I be concerned with the little pieces of fruit on the lowest branches of the human tree because the same root nourishes us? What is a Hobgomadad to me or I to a Hobgomadad that I should weep for him? Oh, I realize that these little bushmen in the heart of Australia are among my poor relations, a few centuries back—a distinction which I share with the Cabots and the Lodges—but if that is the only link there is between us, I must confess that I feel emotionally closer to an airedale. When I see a good dog, it is love at first sight; but I cannot say how long it would take me, even to get used to a Hobgomadad. And right here in this same town, breathing the same atmosphere of patriotism, culture and fog, many a Protestant, Jew and Catholic feel the same way toward one another.

At this point we should perhaps establish the similarity between racial and religious persecution and the necessity of considering both tonight. Where prejudice exists between Catholics and Protestants, the source is almost always religious. In the case of the Jew it is almost always racial. A Protestant in a Catholic country is accepted at once on becoming a Catholic. His children and his grandchildren never have it thrown up at them that they did not always belong. While here in Boston everyone knows that there have always been three chief ways for an Irish-American to rise in the world: first by extraordinary talent (and that is always unusual—even among the Irish); second, by political sagacity (not quite so unusual); third, by apostasy. For from the very beginning the door was open to any Irishman who would give up the Mass. For thus he became that interesting phenomenon known as a Scotch-Irishman, and the Scotch-Irish can become dreadfully nice people. I know some who are not only Daughters of the American Revolution but Daughters of Runnymede and Sons of Noah's Ark and all sorts of things. But the same is not true of the Jew. He faces a different situation. He may better his lot by wealth and talent and the grandeur of his character, but he has not been able in modern times to avoid persecution by changing his religion. The mobs never ask whether or not he is a Christian Scientist. Still, the cases of all three groups can be considered together because the radical difficulty—group hate—is the same in every case, and group hate is another name for bigotry.

When, now, did this group hate begin? The morning after the first groups were formed—probably before the death of Adam. What is it made of? All the lower human passions, smoldering under a good thick layer of ignorance. Someone has said very well that the ordinary man is down on anything that he is not up on and hates anybody he doesn't know. It may be the hate of contempt or the hate of fear, or just plain, dumb, blind hate. But in any event the first step upwards, the first step toward group tolerance, is to put in order our notions on the important subject of equality.

To avoid, however, a lapse into abstraction let us turn now to your guest of honor, Boston's First Citizen, His Eminence the Cardinal. You think of him as a familiar figure moving about the business of his great archdiocese, clothed in scarlet. His robes are the color of blood, to keep before his mind the blood he is himself ready to shed in carrying out his part in the great commission to teach all nations. With his auxiliary Shepherd, Bishop Cushing, at his side, he tends his great flock of every nationality and race, makes friends of every type of human being, a living example of the proper attitude toward group hate, group tolerance and universal charity. He is himself an Indo-European. I might have said an Aryan, except for its odious implication. More than that, he is a Celt, an American and a Catholic. No one could censure him, therefore, if he admitted that he enjoyed most the company of white American Catholics, preferably if they spoke with a soft, sweet touch of the Boston brogue. In other words, we expect him to recognize the spiritual fact that one religion differs from another in proportion as it contains more or less of the Deposit of Faith; the biological fact that race differs from race and the psychological fact that a man who is not proud of his own race and nationality is not unlike a man who is ashamed of his parents. But I am sure he would go further still. He would admit that the dominant civilization in the world today is still definitely Graeco-Roman, though many other civilizations flourished before the torch was lighted on the Acropolis and some have flourished since, that hence, in a way, some races are superior to others at various times and that at present the white race is supreme; that there are for example more strong men among the Scandinavians than among the Polynesians; there are more educated Europeans than Africans; more wealthy Americans than Chinese—keeping, however, in mind that many blacks and browns and yellows are individually superior to very many whites. And what we say of these five great racial divisions is equally true of all their subdivisions. It would be true even of the Nordic race, if such a thing existed. So that the inequality of races and nations is really the inequality of individual men taken on a percentage basis. And such an inequality is an old story to the Cardinal.

For he was never swept away by the emotional thinking of the French Revolution. He always saw in Jean Jacques Rousseau a dangerous dreamer who built up an ideal—the equality of man—on sentimental rather than on rational foundations. He always knew that no two men are equal, physically, mentally or morally; that aside from the vague fact that all are rational animals, the only true equality among men is a spiritual one which Rousseau would not recognize. To the so-called modern philosophers, however, this thrilling idea of nature, which began by singing the "*Marseillaise*" and plastering France with "*Liberté, Egalité* and *Fraternité*" was at first the ultimate revelation. Disillusionment, however, was not long in coming. The Great Enlightenment, as they called it, proved to be a mere mood, which had to break down in contact with experience. We borrow the word mood from Chesterton, who uses it to keep in mind the essential sentimentality of the thing. For no sound reasoning underlies the *Egalité* of the French Revolution, and this fact, forcing its way into the modern mind, has resulted in a strange perversion. While still doing lip service to the supremacy of the common man, more recent thinkers have proceeded step by step to degrade him from an end to a mere means, a means to something outside of himself.

Take for example the ever-present smug Humanitarians, a group which is often about as human as the Rationalists are rational and the Liberals are liberal. To such the individual man is living not for God, not for eternal happiness, but for mankind, a vague destiny which seems to include empty churches, cold hearthstones and loveless marriage beds. But if in the last century poor individual man escaped the Humanitarians, it was only to become a means to a more specific but equally degrading end, equally outside of himself. The Imperialists, on the one hand, made him live for the good of a government; the Marxists made him live for the good of a class—not even for the good of his own class, but for the good of the merely dominant class, the proletariat. And now we have the latest fashion in human destiny, Racism. Man is now to live for the good of the race. Whatever that means, it follows along with the other paganisms of the century, trampling on the dignity of the individual man, making him merely a unit in the mass and isolating the mass from the rest of the world. This same spirit is now applied to the field of religion as well. No longer interested in the amount of truth a given religion may teach, this spirit is only concerned with creating a new mass into which undistinguishable human beings are to be poured so that they can be hated more conveniently.

Thus has the wheel turned full in 150 years. A movement which began by placing the lowliest man on the loftiest pinnacle ends by dragging down the finest flower of intellectuality and submerging it in a mass—a race, a nation, or a sect. Why? Because from the very beginning the modern mind has missed the real source of man's equality with man. It does not know what makes a Chinese coolie the equal of a Roman cardinal. It is the fact that they were both created by the same God to enjoy Him fully for all eternity, a destiny that dwarfs all accidentals, social, economic, intellectual; a destiny that brings us all not only dignity, but freedom. For if the coolie and the cardinal have the same divinely appointed end, they are equally inviolable with regard to that end and the necessary means of achieving it. Let us add, too, that with the necessary grace they are equally capable of attaining it. They are not, therefore, in the eyes of God, atoms in a mass, marching pieces of proletariat or so many pounds of anti-Semitism or Presbyterianism. They are persons, rational substances, complete and individual. Is it not heartening to us as Americans to realize that what man is before God he is before the Constitution of the United States, a person, not a unit; a rational substance, complete and individual; a spiritual substance that can reason and choose; a unique substance, unlike any other person in the world?

Group hate, therefore, whether it be racism, Marxism, militant atheism, anti-Christianism, or anti-Semitism, strikes at a fundamental concept of our religion and of our patriotism, that all men are equal as persons; that if a given race or nation or sect is for some reason superior to another, no person is for that sole reason superior to another person, for all alike are moving toward a permanent destiny—union with the eternal God.

Men may of course refer to such a point of view as merely a beautiful ideal, but it is more than beautiful, it is sound, and, like all sound ideals, perfectly compatible with realism. It admits the inequality of groups and admits that the intermingling of groups is often detrimental. The Jews, for instance, were once forbidden to intermarry with the surrounding nations because of the gross and foul idolatry that hemmed them in on every side. Other reasons may make a similar policy equally valid today. Again, in the economic field, particular groups may have prior rights in a given locality and may resist the invasion of another group as a householder would a burglar. But we cannot admit any justification for the excesses indulged in under our eyes today, wherein free persons are persecuted because of the sins of other free persons, or, worse still, because the dominant group doesn't like their color or merely desires to plunder them. Even if it be proved that more persons of one group are given to a certain vice than those of another, are more frequently convicted of—let us say vagrancy or violence or extortion—we still protest against group punishment. Put a greater proportion of that group in jail, or banish them if you must, but banish them as persons and do not crucify the splendid men and women who happen to be only racially associated with them.

As a final test of its realism, we have found our old ideal exemplified in the distinguished man whose robes first suggested this line of thought, a very real man, a real American and a real Celt, who loves his country and loves his race, but who does not need the red of his gown to remind him of a greater love than either of these, the love of souls; souls so dear to Christ that He died for them; individual, rational souls in every corner of Boston, in every corner of the earth, men—not mere individuals, but persons.

LUCIFER

ATTITUDINIZING

———◆———

TO MOST OF US THE
DEGRADATION OF GER-
MANY TODAY IS PERHAPS TOO
PERSONAL A THING. WE HAVE
come in contact with individual victims. We have been
outraged by the ruthlessness of individual officials. Yesterday it was a German nun who told me in a voice that
was dull and tired about the sufferings of her starving Sisters. The other day it was a famous scientist who had found
a haven at Fordham, after being dismissed from his own
university, robbed and expelled from his native land, because he had not the mark of the beast on his forehead.
The day before it was a boy of seventeen, a Jewish boy of
remarkable promise, saved from a grotesque fate by a fellowship in an American university.

Hearing these individual cries of pain day after day has
brought the situation so close to us that we can readily lose

our perspective. We may sometimes recall the obvious political significance of a spectacle which shows the destruction for other people of all that we cherish in this ever more dear United States, but we nearly always forget an eternal significance that reaches back beyond our Constitution and Bill of Rights. We miss the forest looking at the trees.

For the situation in Germany today is not merely political or economic. It is true that fantastic autocrats dread the return to normal times; they need fire and smoke as a background for their attitudes. It is true that extravagant militarists have to resort sooner or later to confiscation of private property; hence the $400,000,000 fine on a crushed and demoralized people.

But there is an influence at work in the Third Reich mightier and more sinister than greed for either place or gold. What Cardinal Faulhaber can see tonight through broken panes of glass is the same influence that St. Jerome saw through his tears when they told him that Rome was burning, the same influence that was sweeping over northern Africa when Augustine turned his face to the wall and died. For Alaric is back and Genseric and Attila, the Hun, Attila, who called himself the scourge of God—except that the first Attila had never been a Christian, had never partaken of the sacraments. The early Huns had always been barbarians. The fact that the National Socialists were born in a civilized fatherland, a glorious Germany, rich in cultural traditions, dotted with churches whose lovely painted windows shone with German saints—this fact gives the present campaign of frightfulness a very profound significance, a significance as profound as hell.

For here we see another fall from grace. Here again we see the perfect flower of pride: the love of self even to the contempt of God, to the contempt of God's other children; the hardness and cruelty that has always characterized a pagan society. For official Germany first went pagan and then went mad—through pride.

Lucifer, you remember, once tried to play the God before the eyes of the true and infinite God. He struck an attitude so grotesque, so hideous, that nothing remained but to sweep him away into darkness, his whole glorious being distorted, perverted, ruined. This former angel, this Prince of Light, once he let his pride fully master him, became so foul that even the swine of the Gerasenes committed suicide rather than associate with him; and the National Socialists have let their pride master them fully.

So that, when we read the bitter and disgraceful news day after day, when we see the broken lives that are washed up on our shores, we share in the sorrows of the individual victims; we burn with resentment as Americans, before this spectacle of tyranny, but we see beneath it all the deep significance that Augustine saw when he wrote of the City of Pride and the City of Love. Pagan barbarism has again raised its head in Christian Europe, but this time it is a barbarism that has apostatized from Christianity and thus has learned to burn and loot and slay with a malice unknown to more simple savages.

ART AND

TRADITION

———◆◆———

WHEN THE FOUNDERS
OF THE METROPOLITAN
RECEIVED THEIR CHARTER FOR "A
MUSEUM AND A LIBRARY OF ARTS,"
the United States probably deserved the reputation it had
in the capitals of Europe. It was high noon for us in the era
of the Golden Cuspidor. General Grant was in Washington
when he wasn't in Long Branch, and Mr. Tweed was in
New York. So that all the boys of both the major parties
were doing better than the artists of the time. Newport was
in its red-brick infancy and local society had still a long
time to wait for grand opera and Mrs. Astor's plush horse.
However, really elegant people went to Europe for their
culture and on their return brought home with them as
much European elegance as they could carry, chiefly paintings in enormous gold frames and allegorical sculpture.
From this it was an easy step for a group of leaders to ar-

range a public exposition, their purpose being to elevate
the subnormal taste of those who could not get to Europe
for an elevation. Actually, as so often happens, these philan-
thropic men and women builded better than they knew.

Their first end they achieved. Because of the Museum
they founded, public taste has been immensely improved
over the years and the once patronizing Europe now looks
to Mayor O'Dwyer's city as the capital of many different
arts. Because of the inspiration given by this museum, our
homes and our churches, our furniture and our jewelry, even
our industrial designing and commercial advertising have
made American life more livable, more gracious. And yet,
impressive as this contribution has been, it is small compared with what is now expected of this great university of
popular education. For now issues have arisen of greater
moment than public taste. Now Western Civilization has
reached its hour of decision and people of the iron age and
people of the stone age are closing in on modern man. Now
modern man himself, the heir of Greece and Rome and
the Mount of the Beatitudes, is losing not only his sense of
inheritance, but with it his sense of identity, his sense of
direction and his hope in the future. Because, as Maritain
says: "We have destroyed our past and lost its sense of
values." We have lost our sense of present values too—
moral, intellectual and esthetic values. This, then, is the
challenge that faces your trustees and directors on the eve
of your diamond jubilee. Can they range this immense ar-
tistic power—the greatest in the new world and one of the
half-dozen greatest in the entire world—on the side of the

church, the court of law and the college of liberal arts in a desperate struggle to keep open the channels of tradition? How much we need the past is obvious. All true civilization is 90 per cent heirlooms and memories, an accumulation of small but precious deposits left by the countless generations that have gone before. Only very proud or very ignorant people imagine that our muddle-headed present can afford to begin everything all over again every day and invent for each succeeding group a new alphabet, a new multiplication table, a new code of laws, a new humanism and a new religion. And yet there are so many of them shouting at us from the printed page!

Nothing, it seems to me, could be a more painless remedy for a fatal bias like theirs than an intelligent visit to the Metropolitan Museum of Art. It can leave with them in such a short and pleasant time the same conviction that years of study or years of travel would give—the conviction that sublimity is within the powers of man as man and genius is not confined to any age or place. Whether it be the granite head of "The Great God Amun," or "The Hunt of the Unicorn," or the Rospigliosi cup, or lovely paintings on silk and vellum and canvas from China and Persia and every part of the civilized world, there is a constant reminder here that man always was at least half angel; that in every century from the first page of his prologue, in spite of cruelty and oppression and corroding selfishness, man has always been capable of loving not only God but God's beauty mirrored in all the beauty of the world. Human beings have always been capable of humanism as well as of religion, though, being weak, their enthusiasm for both tends to rise and fall with the wavelike movements of history.

You probably remember the great gentleman and scholar of the ninth century, Lupus, the old Abbot of Ferrières. In his study of literature he was struck, as many have been since, by the recurring cycles of greatness, first in Greece and then in Rome, and coined a happy phrase to describe the phenomenon. He called it "the growing green again of letters." So, too, after a few hours in this museum, this Temple of the Muses, we begin to sense that power of resurrection in the affairs of men, that spirit of eternally recurring spring. We begin to believe that in spite of all evidence to the contrary, men even today in the atomic age can achieve new heights of culture and morality, though the culture and morality will not be new. Enduring humanism and eternal religion will merely be growing green again.

The major responsibility for the resurgence of religion may lie in other hands than yours—though even in this you have a minor part to play—but in the returning springtime of the arts which a mechanized and arid world is longing for, who can better lead the way than you? Who can point out more vividly the essential fact that a resurgence of humanism, like peace itself, will depend on the mutual esteem of civilized peoples? As it is, Greece has been forgotten, Italy and Japan are despised. No effort is made to understand Spain. Germany, Austria, and Poland are geographical expressions. England is a poor relation, France a nuisance, and the little nations never mattered anyway. With nothing left, therefore, worthy of our attention but Stalingrad and Pittsburgh, we need more than ever to bathe our souls again in the light that shines over the centuries from Athens, Florence, Paris, Madrid, Antwerp. We need to look upon the glory of Raphael, Memling, Velasquez, Donatello, Dürer, El Greco, Rembrandt. We need to realize, more deeply than ever before, that two great brotherhoods transcend all national boundaries, all chasms of color and race; that men can be brothers not only in the love of God but in the love of eternal and universal beauty.

All this is an old story to your farsighted trustees and directors. They realize fully their responsibilities. They are eager as ever to fulfill the first intention of the founders and continue to improve the public taste at home. But they are more eager still to take up this new challenge that the war has left at their door—to use the universal language of art as a means to foster mutual respect among the civilized nations of the earth and to build up in the souls of our own people hope and faith in the brave new world to come.

And for all of this they ask from the public no more than the price of the bombs that were dropped in a single night raid over Tokyo.

THE JESUIT
ENIGMA

———◆———

WHEN YOUR VENER-
ABLE RECTOR PRESSED
ME INTO SERVICE AND INFORMED
ME IN HIS MASTERFUL WAY THAT
I was to speak this morning on the 400th Anniversary of
the Jesuits, I got down the dictionary to see just what they
were. I had known a few in my time, but it is difficult merely
by knowing thousands of Jesuits to discover their mysterious individuating notes. It is even true that I've been one
myself for twenty-seven years, come Michaelmas; not a mere
blue apron, mind you, but a thirty-third degree, right in on
all the plots—and yet, I feel that something must have elud-
ed me. For according to the dictionary, Jesuitism consists of
using craft or insidious arts or practices—and despite a lively
interest in detective stories, I've never yet been able to catch
my brother Jesuits red-handed. So I suppose, if you really
want to discover what they are up to, you will have to read
the pious ejaculations of the sixteenth-century reformers, the

temperate pronouncements of Jansenists in the seventeenth century and Rationalists in the eighteenth, and, especially, the dignified and judicial charges of the Bourbons, who had them suppressed in France and Portugal. Of course, in spite of the evidence, they have always had friends; they must have some even today. Right here in the Metropolitan area, for example, they have eleven thousand students enrolled, and at least twenty-five thousand persons attend their churches. But you know as well as I do that every time there is an enlightened government, every time a group of real liberals comes into power in a Catholic country, like the Russian Loyalists in Spain or the Grand Orient in France or the glorious revolutionists in Mexico and Central America, known to all the world for their personal integrity and unselfish patriotism—what does such a government do? It banishes the Jesuits. First thing! Even before it proceeds to the more important business of liquidating the Church. Out they go! Or rather out they pretend to go. Actually they contrive to slink around corners with false mustaches and red neckties, looking for all the world like the most enlightened liberals and eventually come back and start all over again. The Order in the last four hundred years has been buried by its enemies almost as often as the Catholic Church itself, but the difficulty is that these liberals have never been able to find tombstones heavy enough to keep either of them down. Is it any wonder, then, that outsiders are always puzzling their heads about the secret and power of the Jesuits, trying to solve the Jesuit enigma?

Admittedly, it is a complicated thing, but the two elements that come closest to solving the enigma are, I think, the flexibility of Jesuit administration and the reckless devotion that every true Jesuit feels to the folly of the Cross.

The first of these we find embodied in the Constitutions of the Society; the second in the book of Spiritual Exercises. In point of importance as well as of history, the second comes first. For every single development of the Society in the last four hundred years can be traced through its extraordinarily adaptable Constitutions to one meditation of the Spiritual Exercises, the Meditation on the Kingdom. For when St. Ignatius arose from his knees in the Cave of Manresa, he said very quietly: *"Domine, ego sequar te ubicumque ieris"* —and that was the first rough blueprint of the Order. To the world, as you know, he seemed a man of shrewd sagacity, sound judgment, boldness and determination; a man of dominating personality who had externalized himself into the Company he had founded. But from the beginning, the world has seen only the husks of reality. The last thing Ignatius thought of was externalizing himself. The last question he asked himself, if indeed he ever asked it, was "What is my will in the matter?" At a time when poor, distracted Europe was bursting into fragments because every man was trying to impress his opinion on the rest of mankind, this Spanish soldier realized that the hour's need was not only the Way and the Life but, more than either, the Truth. And so, in everything he did, his eyes were fixed upon the Eternal Truth. As he limped about the streets of Rome in his patched shoes and worn cloak, he was known to the little children as "the lame man who always looks at the stars." But to those who lived with him night and day, that gaze of his went far beyond the stars. He always seemed intent upon the crucifix, trying to read the lips of his Redeemer.

When the time came, then, to define the particular end of the new Society, it wouldn't particularize. Its end was the Greater Glory of God, through the salvation of souls, and its means were as flexible as its end was general. Any work assigned by the Holy Father at any time was to be its particular work. The Company was always to remain fluid—the light cavalry in the army of Christ. Apparently they were looking for travel and variety and they certainly got it. You have often heard what they did at the Council of Trent. As sons of Xavier, you know every step in the brilliant and ecstatic life of your patron, the Apostle of the Indies. You have heard how some of the early Jesuits became mandarins and some became coolies, how some were brahmins and some pariahs, how some were the confessors of kings and some were the slaves of the Mohawks, how some were astronomers, mathematicians, playwrights and poets. But do not imagine from this that their lives were always brilliant or romantic. There is more than one way to reap a harvest, and much of their work was and is just plain humdrum heroism, though worked out on the same plan as the colorful life of Xavier.

Inevitably, however, an Order of this sort whose avowed aim was to furnish the Church not merely with teachers or merely with preachers or merely with anything else, but with a variety of types that could fit any emergency, an Order whose government allowed for adaptation to the most extraordinary circumstances, a machine which like a one-part

tool was too simple to break down, was sure to arouse various emotions in various camps, the admiration of some, the
jealousy of others, the suspicion of the rest. Because they
were lawyers and knew their way around the courts, the
Jesuits were "prevaricators"; because they wanted no digni-
ties and were trusted by popes and kings, they were "politicians"; because they knew their moral theology scientifically,
they were "hair-splitters"; because they were popular confessors, they were "laxists"; because they knew their dog-
matic theology, they were "bigots"; because they were soldiers and obeyed at the least sign of their superior's will, they
were "fools."

It always appealed to their sense of humor when their
enemies found them crafty and insidious, for a baffled adver-
sary who sputters because he doesn't know the answer is always funny, but from the beginning these strange men loved
to have the world call them fools. They loved to feel that
they carried in their hearts no mere symbol of Christ's folly,
but the very folly itself that took Peter to the Cross in Rome
and Thomas to the sword in India. Even today they love to
feel that they are filled with the selfsame foolishness that
passes for wisdom in eternity. They are never flattered to be
known as business men, and, to tell the truth, I've known
very few who were! But reckless idealists, spendthrifts for
Christ—that's another thing.

Let us take for example the missionary work of our own
Province. What is it I ask you but foolishness, after all,
when capable men who have devoted their young years to
science and literature, to philosophy and theology, set out on

a journey of nine thousand miles to teach the Filipinos the meaning of the Crucifix? Yet that is what it comes to in the last analysis. They may open schools and colleges and observatories and seminaries and hospitals and chapels, but all their activity will spring from one simple objective—the preaching of Christ and Him crucified. There you have in its bare essentials the foolishness for which these fools of Christ are giving up their lives. And not one little group alone. They go to join an army, an army of nearly four thousand other Jesuit missionaries doing the selfsame thing in every Godforsaken—or had I not better say, man-forsaken—part of the world. That may be news to those who think of us as a teaching order. For it means that one out of every four available Jesuits is now in the foreign mission field and the other three can be sent any time without warning or consultation.

To the world it is just one more aspect of the old Jesuit puzzle. The world can make nothing of an order which is supposed to be clever—preternaturally so—and still wastes a quarter of its most active men on this trifling visionary business of the missions. Think of it! Four thousand trained men working overtime to get simple, ignorant people— Esquimaux, Africans—to go to Mass and say their beads and make their first Holy Communion! Apparently the Jesuits, like the Bourbons, have learned nothing and forgotten nothing since the seventeenth century when they used to send out their choicest and best to the jungles of India or the woods of Canada. And what did they ever get out of it anyway? They made their converts, millions of them, but periodically they and their converts were put to death. Periodically their enemies in Europe undid all their work. Too bad they hadn't learned a thing or two from the early settlers of New England. There were men of sense for you—men of the world—and the world still honors them, affectionately. They, too, made contacts with the backward races, but except for a few John Eliots, they knew better than to waste the Gospel on them. They specialized in rum-running and the capture of slaves. So that when their ships sailed back to their rock-ribbed Puritan homes, they had never lost a man by crucifixion. They hadn't lost a silver pound. On the contrary, their missionary labors had yielded them enough to build up colleges and gain control of the nation. But as for the Jesuits, they have not only been wasting their time abroad, they have been crippling their work at home. Now that's an interesting charge. Let us see if there is anything in it.

Let us again take our own little Province, for example—the Maryland-New York Province. We have at present living within four states about one thousand five hundred men, of whom more than half are still in their studies and many more are old and infirm; that means that about four hundred and fifty men are carrying a load which includes two universities, four colleges and ten high schools, with a total registration of about twenty thousand students—a work which obviously should call for many more Jesuits than we have. But the same little group of four hundred and fifty is also responsible for the publication of six periodicals, including *America, Thought* and the *Sacred Heart Messenger.* They are, besides, taking care of eleven city parishes, twenty-eight country churches and a number of chaplaincies. In the course of the year the same men give about one thousand five hundred retreats and novenas and missions and hear about two million confessions. This is not said in a spirit of boasting. We have nothing to boast about. If we were all saints, as we should be, we could do five times as much as we do. But it serves to sharpen this necessary point in the argument. We are handicapped in man power. We could use twice the number that we have—many of our best men are burning themselves out before their time, and still this one Province has two hundred and fifty men in the field of the Foreign Missions. Men enough to staff five more schools like Xavier, or two more universities like Fordham.

Do you see now why the world calls us fools? And do you see why, if we use its own standards, we must admit it is right? We must admit that no certified accountant could make sense out of our business. But then, no certified accountant could balance our divine Lord's books, where all the credits are debits and all the debits pure gain, where the business deals with souls, where each item purchased is worth more than all the material equipment of our corporation. Such bookkeeping calls not for higher, but for the highest mathematics—the mathematics of the angels, who are used to God's ways of reckoning things. God's mysterious ways! For there is a mystery about them, even after all the hints we have had from the saints and the prophets. It takes a chosen soul to realize the balance of eternal loss and gain —the contradictions involved in spiritual values. Still we can all see dimly as in a glass—so let us, handicapped as we are, examine the folly of Christ but with eyes of Faith.

The Diocese, you say, and the Province, are suffering a loss in man power. But are there any proportionate gains? There certainly are. There are treasures of grace given in exchange, some of them very palpable. In the Diocese, for instance, the faithful are constantly reminded by the thought of the missions, as Pius XI, the Pope of the Missions, reminded them in his Encyclical on the Sacred Heart, that theirs is a Catholic Church, not a narrow parochial sect; that their interests are as wide as Christ's; that they are themselves, clergy and people alike, the fullness of Christ, the members of His Mystical Body, and Christ is priestly in every member; that Christ by His Priesthood is the Redeemer of man and, in mysterious union with Him, you and I continue the work of Redemption; that men are to be saved by other men, that is, by us. That realization alone is a leaven of spirituality that affects every work in the Diocese, so that where the mission spirit is strongest, the best influence of the Church is felt!

That explains, too, why religious orders flourish with vocations in proportion to their reckless generosity. It is of course their supernatural reward—their hundredfold—but part of the explanation is perfectly natural. For young men of a certain type are always attracted to a life that looks like a challenge. They want something that will call for idealism and courage and when they give themselves up they want to feel the sacrifice. We know, gentlemen, at our age, what chance there is for sacrifice right here at home; what chance there is for crucifixion in the drabbest private lives. But thus accepting a dim vague cross supposes a mature and settled personality. Youth wants clear bright colors and sharp lines of experience, even in its suffering. This is the spirit, naturally speaking, that attracts them to a missionary order. This is the spirit they bring with them into the cloister and nourish there with manly piety. In their novice days they have, like St. Teresa, a secret hankering after "Moors and martyrdom" that never really leaves them while they keep a spark of the first inspiration. There may be a little touch of adventure and romance about it, but what harm if there is, since there is plenty of logic too? For every one of them at the outset made a good retreat—a long retreat. He meditated then on man and sin and death and hell; for weeks he studied the beautiful soul of our Lord and Savior and when he finished it all he whispered with absolute sincerity the very words that St. Ignatius whispered to himself: *"Domine, ego sequar te ubicumque ieris."*

He saw Christ standing shoulder deep in the autumn fields, His eyes fixed eternally on the souls of men; he heard Him say to His Apostles, "The harvest indeed is great." He saw Him by the lakeside giving the Eleven their mission and the mission of the Catholic Church: "Going therefore teach ye all nations." And how can a man be satisfied when there are harvests still unreaped, nations still untaught, still unbaptized?

The sacrifice, then, of these missionaries of ours whom we have taken as examples, their Christlike folly, means much for the East and for Rome, as well as for their own Diocese and Province. But what does it mean for you and me? When I stop and think of men who were novices with me, who studied at my side for fifteen years, who played with me, swam with me, went on hikes and picnics, men who like all the things I like—good reading, good music, good company, good living—and I realize that they are quartered now in grass huts in the wildest part of the country, with more work than any man can do, and not always the necessities of life to do it with, such realization is a tonic that makes any sort of work seem light. And when I realize that some of them are in the leper islands of Cebu and Culion, year in, year out, with those poor rotting outcasts who have been sent to the Islands to die, the thought of them is a lens that focuses my ordinary day and puts all my ridiculous troubles into their proper perspective.

But above and beyond all that, what is the greatest thing they do for every one of us personally, not excluding the Most Reverend Archbishop and the Holy Father himself? They cheer us—they fill us with courage and pride by the spectacle of a good square blow dealt right over the heart of the world—that world that Christ refused to pray for. What a perfect rebuke it is to this rotten spirit around us, with all its vanity, its selfishness, its sensuality and its pride, when thousands of men toss aside with a smile everything that the world loves, when thousands of young men lay down their lives, without posing or self-pity, for a great ideal. It strengthens our Faith when we see that our Faith is still worth dying for. It strengthens our hope in the Kingdom. But it is the sight of their charity that will make even us other Christs. Of course I am prejudiced, but you know sometimes I think St. Ignatius would still recognize his Company even after four hundred stormy years.

LABOR
AND THE
PRIESTHOOD

———◆———

I NEVER TOOK PART
IN A CELEBRATION
WHICH I CONSIDERED LESS REMARK-
ABLE THAN THIS EVENING'S. IT
reminds me of the story they tell up in Buffalo, the Queen of
the Great Lakes, about a literal-minded Englishman who
was taken out by one of the natives to view Niagara Falls.
They stood on Artists' Point in silence for a few moments
until the Buffalonian burst out with local pride: "Have you
ever seen anything so remarkable as all these floods of water
tumbling into the abyss?" Said the Englishman: "I see nothing remarkable whatever in their tumbling. After all, what's
to prevent them?" In like manner, I can see nothing remarkable in the fact that a Catholic priest should have devoted
the best years of his life to special problems, particularly to

labor relations, and still less that, being the right sort of priest, he was eminently successful. After all, what was there to prevent him? He was carrying out not only the principles of true Americanism, but the dearest wish and explicit instruction of all the modern Popes since the time of Leo XIII. This great Pope of the workingman said repeatedly that priests should excel in their knowledge of social matters and should develop a keen sense of justice to oppose all unjust claims and unjust actions, in all things showing prudence and discretion, but "aglow with the fire of charity." Pope Benedict XV wrote in like vein: "It is our desire," he said, "that priests regard it as one of their obligations to devote themselves as far as possible to social theory and action by study, observation and work and that they support in all things those who in this sphere exercise a wholesome influence."

In these quotations, however, there are no ideas that are really new, only a few new words, just as in Leo's great Encyclical on "The Condition of the Working Classes," the *Rerum Novarum,* known as the Charter of Labor, there is no departure from the traditional principles of the Holy See. Leo was the first Pope to talk about trade unions, open shops and boycotts, for the same reason that he was the first Pope to talk about automobiles, but throughout his monumental document there is the overtone of nearly two thousand years. Priests were always expected to study the problems of the workingman and where as a class they have failed to do so, religion has always suffered accordingly. This does not mean to imply, of course, that all priests have the same particular interests or talents. Only people who have never met any priests think that they are all alike, just as people who have never moved in navy circles think that the eighteen hundred sailors on a battleship are all alike. Priests differ, like all groups of men, according to their time and country and the class of people they have lived with and the kind of mother and father they had. An Irish priest and an Italian priest, for instance, show many interesting variations of type that are sometimes amusing to each other and sometimes not. You have probably heard of the Italian Monsignore who was dispatched to Ireland on a diplomatic mission for the Vatican. On his return a clerical friend asked him how he found the priests in Ireland. "Priests?" said he, "There are no priests in Ireland, they are all Popes." And the Rector of Carrick-on-Shannon, returning to the green fields and the little white cottages of Roscommon, after a pilgrimage to Rome, was heard to remark that all they needed there to make it indeed the Holy City were a few more good Irish Catholics. Even in a single Diocese, the same generation is never poured into the same mould. There were luxury-loving clerics in Milan when St. Charles Borromeo was the cardinal archbishop, and there were saintly priests living in Autun in the time of Talleyrand. But, as in the case of a battleship, where you can always find a few fools and cowards among the heroes, what makes the difference in any generation is the general average struck, and in all the more glorious periods of the Church, the average of the clergy on the basis of their devotion to social problems, and especially to labor problems, has been consistently high. Priests like St. Ambrose, Augus-

tine, Basil, Chrysostom and Jerome were not exceptional
when they thundered against the labor abuses of a pagan
empire. They were the Church speaking when they reminded the great and powerful of their time that the earth
was intended by God for all children of men, that the
surplus goods of the rich belonged to the needy, since one
man had more right to live than another had to enjoy himself. They outlined the basic arguments for a living wage
and laid the foundations for the medieval doctrine that the
price of goods ought to be sufficient to afford the producer a
decent living. They fearlessly taught that the legal possession of property did not always give the owner the right to
do with it just as he pleased, though the right to private
property was a natural right and could not be taken away
from any man. These rights were the new and revolutionary
ideas that came in with Christianity. For in pagan countries
a worker was looked down on as a slave, and even among the
Jews his condition was not much more honorable, until in
the fulness of time, Christ, the great High Priest of the Order
of Melchisedec, came on earth as a workingman and spent
most of his life making oxen yokes and tables and chairs
and beds, common things close to the lives of common people. His first Pope was a fisherman like most of the original
hierarchy, and His Church was the Church where slaves
and freemen met in Sacramental equality. Pope Pius, in
the second century, and Callixtus in the third, had been
slaves themselves before their ordination to the priesthood.
Of course, the old pagan ideals, or lack of them, lasted on
stubbornly for centuries because they catered to the spirit

of the world, but where the Church was strong slavery soon gave way to serfdom and serfdom to liberty. In Ireland, for example, serfdom was ended in 1170, by St. Lawrence O'Toole, and though later the people were physically enslaved by a foreign invader, they never relapsed into the serf mentality. From the time of King John to the present day, the only moral quality that the Irish and the English seem to have in common has been an unshakable conviction of their own natural superiority. In Germany, on the other hand, most of the peasants were still serfs in the time of George Washington, and in Russia there was serfdom until the days of Abraham Lincoln. That may explain, perhaps, why the Absolute State has had such success in Germany and Russia and so much difficulty settling itself in the little green Isle of the Saints. The Irish will not do the goose step for anyone. They prefer to jig and go to church and the church they prefer is still the Church where every class of people can mingle without self-consciousness and, what is more important still, without class-consciousness, either.

It does seem, then, that a man who comes of a stock that has had no contact with serf mentality for eight centuries, who was born and raised in a country where these truths are held to be self-evident, that all men are created equal and that they are endowed by their Creator with certain unalienable rights, who was baptized into the Mystical Body of Christ, a Body of perfect Justice and perfect Charity, who was educated and ordained in a Rome still dominated by the labor ideals of Leo XIII, and who above all lived up to the great expectations that were held of him—it does seem that such a man was a natural for the Labor Relations Board. But of all the qualities and achievements that fitted him for his task, the least was certainly not the fact that he fulfilled the hopes of ordination.

Let us take you back for just a moment to the tenth of June, 1911. We are in Rome, early on a warm, bright morning, kneeling in church with a group of friends and relatives. Before us at the altar the bishop is standing erect, vested with miter and crozier. The archdeacon is just saying in a clear voice: "Let them come forward who are to be raised to the order of priesthood." A group of young men in spotless albs advances to the foot of the altar. One of them is John P. Boland. On his arm are folded the priestly vestments he has not yet the right to wear. He knows how utterly unworthy he or any other man must be to celebrate the awful mystery of Holy Mass and so his eyes are lowered and misty in a manly sort of way, but his step is strong and confident, for his heart is aglow with faith.

As he kneels and bows his head, the bishop crosses the stole upon his breast with the words: "Receive the yoke of the Lord, for His yoke is sweet and His burden light." In God's own time it will seem heavy enough, for trials and failures and misunderstandings lie in wait for him, but heavy or light he will carry it through to the end because it is the yoke of the Lord. Then the chasuble is put on his shoulders with the consoling admonition: "Receive the priestly vestment by which charity is signified, for God is powerful to make you grow in charity and every priestly work." And grow he will as he carries the flame of Christ's love in his breast, lighting little tapers in the hearts of all who meet him, rich and poor, employers and employees.

This, then, is the beginning of a real apostolate. For with the oil of the catechumens on his hands, from thumb to fingertip, John P. Boland, now Father Boland for all eternity, begins a life of arbitration and of judgment. With growing appreciation of his character, we watch him through the years, first a curate and administrator of the parishes of Buffalo, Irish and Italian, and then judge of the Matrimonial Court, handling delicate situations that will make childplay later on of the differences between the A.F.L. and the C.I.O., and finally, on the State Labor Relations Board, as member and as chairman. It has been an extraordinary record calling for many gifts and varied qualities, but, weighing the matter carefully tonight, it seems to this speaker at least that most of his extraordinary success has been due to the fact that he was the right sort of Catholic priest. This humble tribute from a fellow-priest, arranged by Mr. Tuttle, a good Episcopalian, was meant to be symbolic, I am sure. We know the ultimate that is intended when we speak of a poet's poet, of a soldier's soldier and of a man's man. I give you tonight, with deepest admiration, a priest's priest.

HOPE AND
RED HATS

I AM SURE EVERYONE
IS KEENLY DISAP-
POINTED THAT OFFICIAL MOURNING
PREVENTED THE PRESIDENT OF THE
United States from joining us at dinner. Personally, I was
looking forward to an exhibition of tight-rope walking on
the part of our distinguished Republican toastmaster antici-
pating something like the President of The Friendly Sons
of St. Patrick introducing Mr. Churchill. Having sweated
blood to conduct myself all afternoon like a good Democrat,
I was consumed with curiosity to see how the Secretary of
State of the State of New York would eulogize the leader
of the somewhat older Deal. As a matter of fact, when he
heard that the President couldn't come, the toastmaster is
said to have suggested that the junior Senator from New
York make the speech, but the Senator is said to have said
that he was tired of making speeches and the former Post-

master General is said to have said that he doubted that the Senator said it.

But though we regret his absence very sincerely and appreciate the high honor he paid our University this afternoon, it is in a way a relief for the other speakers on the program that the President is safely back in Washington by now. There is so much that one hesitates to mention in the presence of a man who is responsible for every blessed thing that happens in the country, from infantile paralysis to a rainy day. If he were here, we couldn't mention Iran or Paris or Spain. We couldn't refer to ice boxes or bread and butter or soft coal. We should hesitate to mention even the most innocent words for fear of their overtone. They say that the umpires down in the Washington ball park have to yell "Three misses—the batter's out," so that no one will think of John L. Lewis. Actually what I intend to say is innocuous enough to be said in the White House but—who knows?— you might inspire me to an indiscretion before I finish.

It seems only yesterday that we were here in this same room celebrating the Centenary of our Founding in 1841. The Vice President was here, representing Mr. Roosevelt, and I remember calling Mr. Henry Wallace the most popular member of the President's official family. That's how long ago it was! The times were anxious, compulsory military training had arrived, but nobody anticipated Pearl Harbor, then three months away, even those whose business was anticipation. The alumni and friends of Fordham had already subscribed $600,000 of the million that was our centenary goal when war was suddenly declared, and for the next four years our problem at Fordham was not development, but survival. We survived.

And now the war has been fought to the end—to the end of European civilization, but whether we have won or lost remains to be seen. The only thing we are sure of is the truth of the old maxim that in every war bravery is commoner than brains. Our Fordham boys, thank God, had both, and their story as it came to us in press clippings, in letters and conversations with chaplains who had known them or with their ranking officers and companions in the field brought tears to our eyes that we were not ashamed of. Two hundred and eighteen of the dearest and best will never return, and standing a few weks ago in the cemetery of Nettuno, near the murderous Anzio beachhead where four of them fell, I could not help thinking with poor Rupert Brooke, how many lonely corners of the earth would be forever Fordham. A memorial is planned for them on the campus that they loved—not a granite shaft or a sculptured group, not a stadium or a student union, but a century-old University Church rebuilt. At present the only worthy thing we have is a beautiful altar. The rest of the church is a wreck. All the plaster has to come down so the ancient stones can be weatherproofed. Then a panelled entrance will be added and new woodwork throughout, a terrazzo floor and lifesize Stations of the Cross, two side altars as special memorials, a marble floor in the sanctuary suitably inscribed and around the sanctuary walls, where the priest at Mass can read them every morning, panels carved with the golden names of the dead. May their dear young souls rest in peace.

As for ourselves, we meet again for the first time after the storm, and if we look for them carefully enough, we shall find in other meetings that have taken place a few reasons at least for optimism. The gentlemen of the press have met the Soviet in various parts of Europe, west of the iron curtain, and in Manchuria as well. They have been insulted and pushed around and held incommunicado, with the result that factual accounts are now replacing the old romances of wartime. The average American has met Mr. Gromyko, not personally as I have—I blessed his lunch one day to his obvious disgust—but over the radio and through the minutes of the U.N., and admiring fair play and sportsmanship as the average American does, he has no time for the sulking Andrew. Best of all, the State Department has met Mr. Molotov and has begun to realize that groveling at the feet of the Soviet is not the way to achieve co-operation or to further peace. It is also beginning to realize what Mr. Churchill saw some time ago, that, if the Soviet succeeds in drenching Spain with blood—a prospect which Mr. Gromyko anticipates with equanimity—there will not always be an England.

Which reminds me that two months ago the devotion which His Eminence Cardinal Spellman has for his Alma Mater made it possible for me to be in Rome at the Great Consistory. I was there with Msgr. McCaffrey, Joe Lynch and Joe McKee merely because the Cardinal wanted what was dearest to his heart close to him in his great moment:

his family, his Archdiocese, the Roman College and Fordham. We were there as your representatives and our pride
was yours.

We were a little like a fond parent at graduation who
sees only one of the three hundred graduates, but two other
figures caught at least our sidelong attention. One was Cardinal von Galen of Münster, the other the youngest in the
College—fifty years younger than the eldest—His Eminence of Westminster, Cardinal Griffin, who this very day
has become one of us. His first purpose in flying to America
was to become an Alumnus of Fordham, his second was suggested to me by the memory of a Cockney patriot whom I
met when I went to London three years ago to preach in
Westminster Cathedral. One day riding down from Dollis
Hill to Marble Arch on the top of a bus I noticed two unmistakable G.I.s in the front seat. Every time the conductor
came up he would put his arms around them and whisper
a little story in their ears. His stories were evidently huge
successes, so when I was getting off I asked him with my
best Cambridge accent if he had gone to school with the
appreciative young soldiers. "No" he said, "they're Americans and you and I 'ave got to send 'em 'ome friends of
the Empire!"

No personal interest, however, in Cardinal Spellman or
Cardinal Griffin could obscure the central meaning of the
drama that unfolded that day before our eyes in Vatican
City. Here was no mere ceremony, no mere echo of the past.
Everyone present who had made the meditation on the Two
Standards could think of nothing else that morning in St.

Peter's. With atheistic Communism creeping over Europe like delta mud, everyone sensed a new barbarian invasion. They thought of Pope St. Leo the Great who rode out alone to meet Attila the Hun, "The Scourge of God," and armed only with prayer turned back the tide. Here they saw one old man—tall, erect, his black eyes searching as ever— seated on a throne above the tomb of the Apostle, gathering around him from all parts of the earth seventy Counselors, most of them, like himself, old men, and as he placed on the head of each new cardinal a blood red hat, we were not too sure that in every case the color would remain an empty symbol. But we were sure that a hundred or two hundred years from now (what is a century in the life of the Church?), while atheistic Communism would be only a bitter memory for the human race, some successor of His Holiness Pope Pius XII now gloriously reigning would still be placing red hats on the heads of other old men whose parents are still unborn.

This is the optimism of Fordham beginning her second century as a university.

Permissu Superiorum